Thank you for buying me.

HOW RUDE!
Modern Manners Defined

To mark the 75th anniversary of
Waitrose in the John Lewis Partnership

How Rude!
Modern Manners Defined

First published in Great Britain in 2012 by Waitrose,
Doncastle Road, Bracknell, RG12 8YA
www.waitrose.com

ISBN 978-0-9537983-1-5

Set in Baskerville

Printed and bound in Great Britain by CPI Group (UK) Ltd,
Croydon, CR0 4YY

HOW RUDE!
Modern Manners Defined

With a foreword by Lynne Truss
and illustrations by Michel Streich

Waitrose

CALL ME OLD-FASHIONED
by Roger McGough

Call me old-fashioned, but I prefer
The country as it used to be
When good manners were part of the fabric
And there was pride in the community

Front doors could be left wide-open
Children play out in the street
Naughty boys on first name terms
With the bobby on his beat

Teachers were loved and respected
Drivers drove slowly with care
Lost purses invariably handed in
And nobody dodged their fare

On a crowded bus a man would stand
To offer a lady his seat
Vegetables came fresh from the soil
Butchers sold innocent meat

Folk said "please" and "thank you"
Never thought of jumping the queue
In A&E on Saturday nights
Nurses had nothing to do

Girls walked home alone after dark
Without fear of molestation
Gays and blacks in the neighbourhood
A cause for celebration

Call me old-fashioned but I prefer
The country as it used to be
When I wore rose-tinted spectacles
In nineteen ninety-three.

HOW RUDE!

CONTENTS

HOW RUDE!

FOREWORD

AN INTRODUCTION
by Lynne Truss

I have in front of me a cutting from a New York newspaper about a woman observed on a commuter train
shaving her legs on the way to work. For me, this awkward situation sums up modern manners quite nicely:
the woman assuming that a train compartment can be a
bathroom if she chooses it to be; people around her wondering, "Isn't this rude? I don't know how to define rude
anymore, but I think this is rude"; no one daring to object, for fear of the woman asking them what right they
had to tell her what to do. Of course, the story doesn't
specify wet shave or dry shave, which possibly makes a
difference. But I like to imagine she brought aboard the
train a bowl of nice warm water, because then she'd have
had the option of clipping her freshly softened toenails in
public as well.

Do you find yourself wondering, "Isn't this rude?"
more frequently than you used to? Do you long for the
days when you could find the answers to all etiquette
issues in a book such as the Debrett's guides ("A thank-
you letter is not obligatory, although one can be sent
to the Lord Steward of the Royal Household")? Well,

I'm convinced that many people are concerned about the breakdown of common codes of behaviour, and that this concern is stressful. So it's rather marvellous that Waitrose, celebrating its 75th year of civil trading within the John Lewis Partnership, has brought together in this book a splendid batch of writers to explore all the slippages that make modern life so tricky.

Manners are not a small matter. We have to share the world with strangers; conventions make us safe. When conventions break down, we feel lonely and adrift. "Two cheeks or one?" is the excellent title of Jenni Murray's chapter – and it's easy to extrapolate from it. If people aren't even sure how to greet their own friends, what hope is there for us when negotiating more complex social transactions? Yesterday I said "Hello" to a woman who was obviously attracted to my dog. "That's OK," she replied, smiling. Now, obviously this was a benign exchange, but I still walked away feeling quite confused. What had I missed? Why had she said, "That's OK"? Did she think I was apologising to her for something? And if so, what?

I hope you enjoy this book as much as I'm sure I will. There was a perfect moment once in *The Simpsons*, where Bart was placed in an isolation bubble because he was contagious. Marge then told him off for slurping his soup, and he barked back, "Hey! My bubble, my rules!" I've been depressed by that ever since I heard it, and I look to the following pages not only to analyse the problem of modern rudeness but to come up with some original answers to cheer me up. In the meantime, I think I've worked out what people really should have said to the woman on that train in New York. "Excuse me, love, I think you've missed a bit. And can I have that after you, by the way? My armpits are really raggy."

Lynne Truss is a broadcaster, columnist and writer. She is author of the award-winning book Eats, Shoots & Leaves: The Zero Tolerance Approach to Punctuation and Talk to the Hand: The Utter Bloody Rudeness of Everyday Life.

CHAPTER ONE

REMEMBER TO WEAR YOUR CLUB TIE
Alexander McCall Smith, on society's unwritten rules

I spend a lot of time in a remote part of the Scottish Highlands. The Morvern Peninsula is a rather empty, mountainous part of the country, accessible by land only over a single-track road. This road has passing places attached to it at intervals, and these allow drivers to pull in to the side if they see another car approaching. Without these, cars would either meet head-on or be pushed off the road altogether. Nobody would get anywhere, other than by foot, and anyone who knows that part of Scotland would agree that it's frequently far too wet and windy to think about that.

The system works, as do many such systems on roads elsewhere in the world. In Vancouver, where the traffic flowing from West Vancouver into the city centre encounters a bottleneck at Lions Gate Bridge, well-mannered Canadian drivers yield to one another in turn, allowing two streams of traffic to merge into one. There are no lights telling anybody to stop; there is no supervision – it just happens naturally. And the same may be said of walking, boarding a train, or a host of other ordinary human activities. We work out ways of ensuring that we can do what we need to do without bumping into others, treading on their toes, or falling over one another in our rush to get there first. Good manners.

In the case of the Scottish single-track roads, most drivers give a wave of the hand to thank the driver who pulls into the passing place to allow them through. This is usually acknowledged by a wave in return. Again, this is good manners. Sometimes, though, a driver goes through without bothering to do this, or the wave of thanks is not reciprocated. Bad manners.

These are everyday examples, and some would call them rather obvious ones. Of course people are going to avoid bumping into one another – that's only common sense. For every functional custom, another can be found that does not appear to have anything to do with preventing collisions or free-for-alls. What about the notion that men should remove their hats on entering a house? What about the once strictly observed rule in polite German society that one should never use a knife to cut a potato? Or the rule against showing the sole of one's shoes in the Middle East, or the requirement in some African societies that one should never take a gift from another with only the left hand rather than the right hand or both? Many people regard these as merely arbitrary social customs with no moral significance to them at all. A breach of such a custom might incur social disapproval, but may have no significance beyond that. Does it really matter if one uses the wrong knife or fork or burps at the table?

A striking thing about manners is that just about everybody has a view on the subject. Those who practise good manners tend to stress their importance, while those who do not may still hold strong views on the subject, even if it's only to decry the customs or courtesies they fail to practice. Few of us are indifferent to manners, even if we may not have worked out exactly why we think the way we do about them. In what follows, I would like to make some suggestions as to why a group of people such as the authors in this volume think that manners are worth thinking about. So let's start with our early ancestors huddled about their fire, tearing the meat off the bone with their teeth, and, we can imagine, burping – and grunting with their mouths full.

There's a wonderful Hebrew word, *shibboleth*, that lends a certain grace to any sentence in which it occurs. The original use of this term was to do with the parts of plants, but the word itself came to be used as a means of distinguishing one group of people from another: a member of the outside tribe would not be able to pronounce it properly and would therefore be excluded – or often slaughtered – by the members of the inside tribe. Later, the word came to have the broader meaning of being any word or custom that served to establish membership. The use of a particular expression, for instance, or sporting a special item of clothing, could both be *shibboleths* that served to identify the insider. A club tie can be an example of a *shibboleth*. Although the wearer of such a thing may claim just to like the colour of the stripes, his real purpose in wearing it is to signal to others that he is a member of an exclusive group. That message is intended for both the general public and for any other members of the group in question who happen to meet him.

Our ancient ancestors must have developed *shibboleths* at a fairly early stage of their social evolution. Human nature being what it is, we both like and need to live in groups, and the whole point about a group is that it has clear boundaries: some people are members, with all the entitlements that go with membership, while others are not. Social rituals help us to bond groups together: if we do the same things at the same time, then we are bound together by the sense of similarity that this gives us. So if the badge of membership of a group is a common salute, or a common way of addressing one another, this becomes an important way of emphasising that the members of the group are in a close relationship with one another – that they are special. And the creation of such bonds confers an evolutionary advantage on those within the group. If you have friends about you, you are a more effective hunter and less likely to fall foul of the predators, human and animal, who were never far away from those early ancestors.

So manners, in the sense of customs that serve to

stress membership, have a strong foundation in our very nature as social beings. Without them, the groups in which early man lived would have been more vulnerable and ultimately less successful. Later on, as society became more complex, so too did social practices. Distinct classes emerged, and a person's whole life could be determined by the accident of birth into a particular class. It was possible to move upwards or downwards within that structure, but at every point in the journey a person could expect to come up against manners as a defining badge of membership. Manners showed others where you were in the pecking order, and they also served to exclude those who were ignorant of them. Social mobility was not out of the question, of course – principally if one had money – but those who aspired to social promotion would have to learn them: Molière, the great French dramatist, wrote a highly amusing play about this in *The Bourgeois Gentleman*. The hero takes lessons in how to behave in society so that he can gain entry to higher circles: this, of course, has all sorts of amusing possibilities for a great comic dramatist, such as Molière was. Similarly, in that wonderful classic of the juvenile imagination, *The Young Visiters*, Daisy Ashford, the precocious nine-year-old author, has her hero, Mr Salteena (who was described as not being quite a gentleman), take lessons in how to conduct himself in society.

So manners have acted historically as a badge of identity that did two things – one positive, and one negative. The positive thing was that they enabled people to bond with each other and to act co-operatively. The negative thing was that they were a means by which insiders could exclude outsiders, even if the outsider wanted to join them. Manners still do those two things, but, as I shall argue, they do a great deal else besides.

Let's start with the strongest justification for good manners: a rationale for good manners that just about everyone – except, perhaps, the most extreme libertarian or the downright anarchist – will be likely to support. This is the principle of offence, and the proposition that manners exist to stop us causing offence to other people.

Joel Feinberg, a prominent American legal philosopher, wrote a highly regarded – and very far from dusty – series of books called *The Moral Limits of the Criminal Law*. His aim in these books was to identify those situations in which a liberal society is entitled to use the criminal law to prevent people from doing certain things. Some themes within that debate are very familiar – pornography, sexual rights and freedom of speech are all issues that have been widely and exhaustively debated in this context. But another part of his enquiry was concerned with the issue of offence to others, and with the issue of how we distinguish between matters of manners (or informal social control) and matters of law. In looking at this issue, Professor Feinberg came up with a gradated list of offensive actions around the simple business of travelling by bus, an everyday activity in which manners can quite quickly come to the fore.

At the mild end of Professor Feinberg's spectrum are affronts to the senses: the passenger on the bus who has not washed for some time, or the passenger who wears clothing of violently clashing colours. In both cases, our senses are affronted, to the point of mild discomfort. Have we any cause for complaint? Probably not. The world is full of people who could pay more attention to personal freshness and to issues of colour co-ordination. But things get worse. Onto the professor's imaginary bus there gets a group of passengers who proceed to eat a picnic – of fish heads, live insects, and animal sex organs pickled with garlic and onion. Over-indulging in this feast, these passengers are then violently sick. And it gets worse as the journey continues as these unpleasant passengers engage in increasingly intimate conduct under the full view of the other passengers. They also begin to speak offensively, starting with mild expletives of the sort commonly heard on buses (and just about everywhere else) but gradually adding derogatory and inflammatory comments of a racial and religious nature. The bus journey, as one can imagine, soon becomes a journey that none of us would care to make – a sort of Dantean excursion into transport hell.

Professor Feinberg's concern is identifying the point

at which the offence caused to the other passengers becomes so significant that even a liberal society is justi-fied in intervening to stop the conduct – if necessary by invoking the full force of criminal law. That in itself is a fascinating debate, but from our point of view what this example does is to show how offence to others is a spec-trum ranging from the mild to the gross, and that if we are to use manners to constrain such offence, then it may be difficult to identify the precise point at which such constraint becomes defensible. Wearing violently unat-tractive clothing may be seen as bad manners by some, but that is probably not a position most people these days would wish to defend. Yet when it comes to vomiting on a bus and making no attempt to clean up then we are clearly in the territory where invoking good manners is entirely justifiable.

My suspicion is that an offence-to-others-type ration-ale can be found in a very wide range of conduct that is dictated by codes of good manners. Unwrapping sweets or chocolate in the theatre during the performance is bad manners because it affects the enjoyment of the rest of the audience. Not washing out the bath after using a shared bathroom is bad manners because the next user will be offended by the layer of scum he or she sees round the rim; it may be perfectly harmless scum, but none of us really likes the thought of having the scum of others floating around our own bath water. Not putting one's hand up in front of our mouth when yawning is bad manners because most of us don't really like staring into the pink interior of another's mouth. And so on.

Rather more tricky are those examples of bad manners in which the offence rationale is perhaps historically based and no longer immediately apparent. Here we might return to the old German rule about not using a knife on a potato. The rationale for that rule is probably to do with the staining of silver: silver and potatoes do not mix very well. But in an age when cutlery is mostly stainless steel or even plastic, what justification can there be for that custom? Surely there is no justification for making this an issue of manners. Similarly the idea that men should remove their hats when entering a building. Whatever justification there may have been for that in the past it is not immediately apparent today, and that explains why most people today see nothing wrong in keeping one's hat on inside. I recall some years ago when I was a visiting professor at a university in Dallas being told by a colleague that if I wanted to identify authentic Texans in restaurants, I should simply see whether the men were wearing hats while they eat. Apparently eating with one's hat on is a traditional thing for Texans to do, and perfectly good Texan manners too.

So in those instances where manners seem to have nothing to do with causing offence to some sensitivity or susceptibility, then can there be any justification for the manners in question? Possibly. And this may be because observing a requirement of good manners achieves some other important objective.

Now we come to an argument that is probably not going to appeal to everybody, but that I think is a powerful one in favour of paying attention to and encouraging codes of good manners.

We can start at the front door. You and I are approaching the door. You step aside and indicate by a gesture of the hand that I should go in before you. I do so and think: good manners. Now inside, you and I are in a group of four people, meeting for a cup of coffee. One of our number launches into a long and boring story. It so happens that the person telling the boring story is blind. One of the party, looking very bored, stares out of the window as the story winds on. Another, although he knows the narrator cannot see him, intentionally continues to keep an interested expression on his face, nodding agreement from time to time. I think: very good manners.

These examples show that there are times when conduct that is considered good-mannered has nothing to do with offence. I am unlikely to be offended by somebody going through the door before me – as long as I am not tripped up or unduly delayed – and the blind storyteller cannot be offended by an expression of boredom on a listener's face. In both of these examples, though, the person showing good manners is effectively saying: I respect you. And that is a further strong justification for good manners: they show respect for other people. That is good on two counts: it limits the likelihood of social disruption (if people respect one another they are more likely to live together in harmony); and then it amounts to an acknowledgment of the fact that other people exist. The importance of this last rationale can hardly be overstated. Most of the wicked acts of which humanity has shown itself to be capable − and here I mean the really wicked acts (genocide, pogroms etc) − are done by people who fail to acknowledge the full existence of others as people just like themselves. Stalin, Hitler and Mao − three great tyrants of the 20th century − did not acknowledge the humanity of their victims. They were spectacularly bad-mannered − as well as being thoroughly evil.

The arguments above are intended to make out a case for continuing to concern ourselves with manners and to continue to teach them to our children. Unfortunately the idea of inculcating good manners in children is not a very fashionable one, and many parents in the United Kingdom today have neither the time nor the inclination to do it. There still are well-mannered societies where strong emphasis is placed on good social manners, but we are not such a society. This is undoubtedly to our cost, as outbreaks of rioting, violence and other forms of anti-social behaviour proliferate. If there are people in contemporary Britain whose daily lives are made a misery by the threatening and unpleasant behaviour of others – and this is the lot of many who live on sink housing estates – then their suffering can be directly linked to the failure of parents to teach and enforce manners. If children are taught good manners resolutely and insistently, then they are less likely to engage in anti-social behaviour that offends and distresses others. They simply are. This view may be disparaged as being unduly simplistic, but its critics either do not see what is happening about them or ignore the evidence of their own eyes. The streets of a typical British city on a Saturday evening are very different from the streets of Singapore at a similar time. They just are. One reveals a society in which consideration for others has become overwhelmed by crude and drunken behaviour; the other reveals a society which some may consider oppressive but which still values good manners and politeness. The problem is that many people now take the pathological lack of manners in Britain as the norm because they have never had the opportunity to see what the alternative is. Churlishness is by no means universal. Recently in Australia I went into a bar and was astonished when the barman smiled at me and asked me politely what I would like. I realised that I had become so accustomed to grudging and casual behaviour that I was treating it as normal. Also recently at Heathrow Airport I made a small purchase from an electronics shop.

The assistant who served me continued his conversation with a colleague throughout the transaction, never once looking at me or addressing me. I was nothing to him – unimportant. He had clearly never been taught those basic precepts of good manners: look at the people with whom you are engaging; don't speak to others while you are meant to be dealing with someone else; say thank you, and so on.

Manners are the building blocks of the greater morality. If we learn manners and observe them, then we are more likely to be attuned to the requirements of living morally in society, with respect for the major rights of others and with sympathy for their feelings. And that is of immense importance: sympathy for others, one of the foundations of a good life, as understood by the great philosophers through history, including that greatest of Enlightenment figures, David Hume. Manners teach us to have that sympathy for others that is the hallmark of the morally good attitude; they are the fundamental moral habits of the heart. They embody the feeling of respect and acknowledgment that we have for others – that we must have for others if life is to be at all bearable. Good manners, even in the smallest of transactions with others, count. They make sense. We should be encouraging them, teaching them in schools; and practising them ourselves, even if there are times when we feel too tired or too busy to bother – especially then, perhaps. We need more emphasis on manners, not less. Now.

Will this happen? Many doubt it; indeed, it seems that the trend is the other way. Our politicians are becoming increasingly ill-mannered in their attacks on one another. They think that clever; they think that is what we expect. Many teachers refuse to correct the conduct and the speech manners of children, feeling that this is not their role; rudeness is widely practised by those who deal with the public; anything goes when it comes to what can be said or done on the airwaves (as it was in the notorious case in which a BBC broadcaster telephoned, on air, a well-known and much-loved elderly actor and told him he had slept with his grand-daughter); courtesy, as opposed to casualness, is seen as old-fashioned, as quaint. That is our current reality.

And yet, amongst all this crudity, we occasionally glimpse an instance of good manners, of considerate and courteous conduct towards others, and we realise, with a warm flush of optimism, that perhaps not everything is lost: somebody is remembering and that there are straws which can always be clung to, no matter how bad the flood.

Alexander McCall Smith is the author of many novels, including the bestselling The No.1 Ladies' Detective Agency series, short stories and academic works. He was made a CBE in 2007. He lives in Edinburgh with his wife and they have two daughters.

CHAPTER TWO

TWO CHEEKS OR ONE?
Jenni Murray, on meeting and greeting

I'm at a party. It's part business, part pleasure. Some of the features among the sea of faces in front of me are recognisable, others are complete strangers. I work on the principle that there's an unspoken agreement that the form of greeting will be indicative of the depth or otherwise of the relationship. After a moment's hesitation, as I run into a friend or associate, the two of us rapidly compute which of us is to make the decision about how far to take it – is it to be mwah, or mwah, mwah or mwah, mwah, mwah?

The step is made, somewhat awkwardly. My theory appears to be working. Contact with a mere acquaintance generally merits a peck on both cheeks. A slightly closer chum and one peck seems to suffice. The really good mates have no hesitation in hugging to demonstrate their pleasure in re-acquaintance and only the Dutch kiss three times. The French used to be the most enthusiastic exponents of the kissing game – three pecks in the year, circa 1970, when I lived in Paris as a student – but my son, who's just returned from Biarritz, assures me even they have cut it down to two.

With strangers, at least in my age group, it's none of the aforementioned. A hand is simply extended and the shake is exchanged. You can make a pretty accurate judgment of whether you wish to continue the getting-to-know-you process on the basis of that first physical contact. Dry and firm? Good sign. It indicates a positive and confident sort. Should make an interesting encounter. Damp and limp? A warning that it might be a good idea to glance over their shoulder, employing that all too obvious "there must be someone more interesting to talk to" gambit and hoping they have the social grace to get the message, mutter "must circulate" and cross the room to bore someone else to death.

And then I spot Gordon powering his way across the room. Gordon is a business contact – useful, but dull and with no visible indication of ever having been taught the more subtle rules of polite interaction. He's a great bear of a man who likes his drink, would smoke at the party if he were allowed to and has the bucolic appearance of one who spends his leisure time hunting and shooting and enjoys his food as much as he revels in his other vices.

On the greetings scale (which I confess is a theory purely based on my own extensive observations), he should be a two-peck man, indicating the respectful distance that should exist between us. I anticipate an over-familiar smacker and then observe, as he begins to bear down on me, an enormous cold sore covering most of the right side of his mouth.

How to escape? I duck sideways into the midst of a group engaged in animated conversation and join in enthusiastically. Gordon skids to a halt in the space I've left behind like an ungainly cart horse, mystified by the sudden disappearance of its target. He looks around, wild-eyed, as I bend my knees to disappear among the crowd and peek through the narrow gaps among the bodies to plan an untimely, but necessary exit. Party ruined for me.

How did we allow ourselves to adopt a Continental form of greeting that the French have performed perfectly competently for centuries, but which sits extremely ill in the more reserved form of interaction, natural to the cool-tempered, somewhat stiff Anglo Saxon? The French seem to be taught from childhood that a slight brush of the cheek will suffice. Sloppy slobbering is not at all acceptable, a message that seems to have translated rather badly across the Channel.

And why oh why do we want to kiss any Tom, Dick or Harry anyway, when a firm handshake will do the job just fine? I felt mean about ducking Gordon and his possibly infectious imperfection in the way I did, but, frankly, I prefer to have close encounters of the physical kind with only my nearest and dearest. Generally speaking, I know where they've been.

I'm not alone in this loathing of excessively intimate greetings with the most casual associates. Lotte Mullan is set to become a big singing star. She's recently brought out her first album and the blog she wrote about the nightmare of being an intern with two big record companies was spotted by a literary agent, made into a book and will soon be a film. The £2 million she's made from the deal has enabled her to set up her own company and stay in control of her work and her image.

Here's what she wrote about what she'd endured: "Apparently Madonna never hugs anyone – it's a firm handshake or nothing. Unfortunately, when you're an aspiring nobody, you have to be more compliant. There's a bizarre over-familiarity in this business. I wouldn't hug or kiss my bank manager.

"I try to go in for the handshake, but guys nearly always disregard it and pull me in for an awkward, sweaty hug. They seem to have it sussed that this is a groping opportunity and if he extends both hands towards your armpits he's likely to get a fingerful of tit. Prime suspects are middle-aged record label executives."

I would gladly see us return to a more old-fashioned form of greeting. If Madonna does only formal handshakes, I see no reason why the rest of us should not follow suit and see it as the coolest way to carry on. Nevertheless, there are certain relaxations in modern social mores that are undoubtedly to be welcomed. It's quite right, for example, that men should not feel the compulsion to walk on the outside of the pavement in the rain to make sure a lady friend doesn't get splashed by any passing traffic. When it comes to the risk of being splattered with mud, equality is to be expected.

I certainly don't wait for a man to open the door for me, unless he is ahead or half my age. I would deem it my duty to show the same respect to a man if I'm in front or if I'm alongside someone who's disabled or much older than me. Nor would I expect, at the end of a dinner party, for the ladies to be asked to retire to discuss trivia while the men smoke, drink brandy and chew over the important issues of the day. The concept of chivalry, mercifully, is largely dying out and, it's to be hoped, being replaced by good, gender-neutral manners.

The same principle applies when it comes to seats on buses and trains. I'll happily stand up for a pregnant woman or elderly person of either sex and few things infuriate me more than the ignorant little oik who plants him or herself into the last available space and acts as though I – a woman for whom sweet 60, rather than sweet 16 is a more apt description – am invisible.

I know I could risk a knife in the ribs or a mouthful of obscenity in return for never, ever letting such an incident pass unremarked, but I have made it a rule to give as good as I get. So far, I'm unscathed, generally get to sit down and like to think I may have taught one or two tearaways some manners.

Nothing, though, is simple in 21st century social life.

Meeting other people face to face, when it is no longer assumed that there is a set of behaviours on which all agree, is a daily minefield. Increasingly, it seems, we all spend far too much time retreating into the easy comfort of our own homes. It takes no effort of human contact to lounge on the sofa watching people being rude or abrasive on television or to cosy up in front of a computer, making connections which are anything but face to face.

For a long time I resisted Facebook. What an artificial environment it is, where value is added to your social kudos by the false assertion that you have hundreds of friends. Most of us have very few people we could truly describe as friends. To boast of hundreds on a social networking site demeans the true meaning of the word.

So, what is a real friend? It is someone you know intimately. It's a person you can trustingly tell your secrets. It's a person you can call on when you're in real trouble, who will always turn up to bail you out. It's someone you see frequently because you love to discuss a film or play with them over a post-show drink or you like to meet each week in a favourite restaurant for a good gossip and a couple of hours of making each other laugh and putting the world to rights.

After much agonising over whether or not to subscribe to a world of meaningless virtual "friendships", I finally succumbed when my children began travelling the world. Basically, I became a stalker (with their permission, of course) and found it deeply reassuring to follow their adventures through the photos they posted regularly. But as a means of communication – unless you're planning a riot or a revolution – Facebook is a complete washout.

A Facebook "friend", with whom you never considered making a meaningful friendship and may merely be a distant relative who merits only a Christmas and birthday card, writes a few words of nonsense on their wall. I have a nephew who's posted, "Northwich Victoria 2: Manchester United 1", a chum who shares, "Dover sole. Yum! Yum!", a goddaughter who announces, "Dinner with Tulisa and Little Mix tonight", and friends of hers who comment: "Brilliant" and "Aw, so cute". Frankly, I'm not entirely sure who Tulisa and Little Mix are, having no interest whatsoever in *The X Factor*, I couldn't care less what Lucy is cooking for dinner and football leaves me completely cold.

Similarly Twitter. Now I was really reluctant to sign up to this. Twitter! It seems to say all we need to know about how little value we place on contact with our fellow human beings. Yes, it's useful for promoting your radio programme or the publication of the paperback version of your new book. It can also come in handy when groups of like-minded individuals want to create the impression of fellowship.

When my entire family went off to New Zealand to watch the Rugby World Cup in 2011, three weeks in advance of my own trip to join them, I found myself curled up alone in my sitting room, scaring the dogs as I shrieked my horror at the pathetic performance England were displaying on the field in Dunedin, and found the only outlet for sharing my disappointment was Twitter. (I joined on account of colleagues at work who felt I was letting the side down by not taking part.)

It's not difficult to express, "Oh my god, is Jonny Wilkinson wearing lead boots?" in 140 characters or fewer, but any sense that the people who ping off their agreement represent anything but an illusion of shared experience and friendship is ridiculous. It's simply not real.

There is one group of Twitterati who do perform a useful function if you can count yourself a member of their club. They are a group of female journalists and writers, ranging from Caitlin Moran at *The Times* to Suzanne Moore at *The Mail on Sunday* and *The Guardian*, who post their articles online, share snippets of gossip, make comment on whatever TV programme they're watching and, earlier this year, raised one of the most irksome and possibly dangerous aspects of the virtual world.

If you stick your head above the parapet and make yourself known as a woman with opinions you're not afraid to express, you will, inevitably, need the agility to duck the crossfire of criticism. In the past there would be letters, generally polite in nature, offering an articulate and, most importantly, signed analysis of where the correspondent considered you were misguided.

What the Twitter journalists revealed – and it was not news to me as I've suffered my fair share of it – was that online comment boards were in danger of silencing young women, perhaps with thinner skins than the one I've developed over the years, because anonymity has allowed criticism to go way beyond what might be considered constructive.

I've been described as Jabba the Hutt (a reference to my ample proportions) and repeatedly told I look "bloody awful with that stupid carpet over your shoulder". It's actually a series of rather beautiful pashminas and woven scarves and I won't be changing my style because some unnamed idiot is allowed full poisonous flow on a newspaper's website, but the young journalists told us of far more offensive and frightening posts.

They had read threats to rape or maim them and constant disapproval, in the most vulgar terms, not of their opinions, but of their appearance. It's a style of verbal abuse from which young men seem to be spared, but which the young women say they find so terrifying it almost makes them afraid to continue in their chosen career.

The anonymity offered by new technologies is what is really changing the way we interact with each other. It has enabled the release of so many people's inner poison pen and leads to a general air of mistrust. If seemingly ordinary people can be thinking the kind of things they spew out online, how can we trust they're not thinking equally evil thoughts when we meet them in person?

It was a matter of some discussion when my friend Joanne decided she had exhausted all conventional routes to finding herself a fella and turned to the internet. She was in her fifties, long divorced with grown-up children, but found herself one of a number of middle-aged women on the pull, with very few opportunities to encounter suitable men who weren't already married and simply seeking a bit on the side.

We established rules. She would agree to meet potential suitors only for afternoon tea. That way she wouldn't have to endure any no-hopers for too long. She would choose a venue in the middle of the city that she knew would be busy. She would never give out her address or her place of work until she was satisfied the guy was not an axe murderer and she would always tell me or one of her other close friends where she was going and when she could be expected back. She would never leave the house without her mobile phone.

It went on for months. She encountered the 70-year-old who'd claimed 50 and whose photo had shown a man with teeth and hair. He had neither. She met the grubby, the smelly, *The Sun* reader whose profile had mentioned *The Guardian*, the inarticulate, the depressed and the one who came to tea asking for a double gin when he'd obviously already had far too many of those over lunch.

She began to despair of ever finding a man who knew good manners required you turn up for a date in clean clothes, having first showered, and with something interesting to say. And then, out on a job – she runs her own company – she met Stephen. Right age, good looking, funny, educated, engaging, comfortably off and a widower. Reader, she married him. Our belief that there were still men around who knew how to carry on an engaging conversation was restored and we adopted the mantra: "Maybe you have to kiss a lot of frogs before you find your handsome prince!"

Which brings us back nicely to the vexed subject of kissing. And, if we're looking to establish some rules for new modern manners, the abolition of the haphazard, stressful and frequently unpleasant habit of pecking perfect strangers on the cheek must be the number-one priority. Madonna has it right. We should proffer the hand, keep the face well back and kiss only the people we love.

We should never perceive social media as a means of communication. It's fine to text that the train is late or ask your child what time they're going to be home. It is not fine to txt yr grnny a hpy bthdy. Similarly with email, I can send brief updates about important news to my son in New Zealand, but the only real means of communication is in a heartfelt letter which he can keep or a long phone conversation during which I can hear the joy or sadness in his voice. And it is not acceptable, although I've done it and regret it, to send sympathy or congratulations by email. Only a carefully chosen card with a handwritten message will suffice.

When it comes to the matter of the danger of anonymous threats or damaging criticism on the internet, newspapers and broadcasting organisations should shut down their message boards unless they can afford to employ someone full-time to carry out careful monitoring and filter out the nasty stuff. Why should readers or listeners be given free rein for their vile bile with no risk of any comeback?

Similarly, children should be taught in school that new media carries inherent risks. Teachers need to make sure their pupils know what bullying online is about before they fall into the trap of using the cloak of anonymity to become a perpetrator or, indeed, to become a victim. And no school should fail to prepare its youngsters to "read" the media that surrounds them. Media studies should not be about how to become Cat Deeley, but how to understand the message and how to employ the usefulness of the internet without falling prey to its perils.

I'm also a great believer in the kind of lessons that were common in my era, that taught us the art of conversation. We would be given a newspaper to read and asked to choose a topic. We paired up with someone else in the class and had 15 minutes in which to converse, discuss or even argue with each other.

When my partner joined officer training in the Navy, he and his fellow juniors were given small-talk lessons. It was essential training for kids who had never before had to attend a cocktail party – a requirement of the job – and, I confess, he has always been much better than me at facing a bunch of strangers and making each one feel at ease by asking them questions about themselves.

What we need to emphasise in the modern world is that, as everything becomes so fast – a message can go around the world in seconds – we must slow down. The real value of close and comforting human relations depends on time. Family and true friends. Old fashioned? Yes. Worth regaining? Without a doubt.

Jenni Murray is a writer and the presenter of BBC Radio 4's Woman's Hour. In 1999, she was made an OBE for services to radio broadcasting and in 2011 she became a Dame. She lives in London and the Peak District with her partner. They have two grown-up sons.

CHAPTER THREE

PLANES, TRAINS AND MOBILES
Sue Perkins, on behaviour in public places

Let me begin by concluding (I'm contrary that way.) Here, in a single sentence, is what I believe to be the real issue regarding the question of manners. Unfortunately, it isn't my sentence, it's a quotation from the eminent American essayist Ralph Waldo Emerson: "Fine manners need the support of fine manners in others."

Says it all, really, doesn't it? Let's take a few examples. In a democratic election, you can't Tipp-Ex out the names of your competitors leaving yours the only one unsullied on the ballot paper. In boxing, The Marquess of Queensberry Rules work only if the other guy isn't holding an Uzi. In chess, you can sustain the tension if pieces move only in the regimented, time-honoured fashion. There's simply no point in you duly pushing your pawn forward a square if your opponent decides to pilot it through the air and dive bomb your king. For the delicate etiquette ecosystem to work, we all have to play by the rules. No exceptions. One size fits all. No running, no bombing, no petting.

This proves to be particularly challenging when travelling on public transport, where the rules of engagement are unclear. Without adequate signage, or historical precedent, we don't necessarily all agree on what is sacrosanct. It's not like the arrangement of knife and fork, or the correct way to pass port – where centuries have chiselled the correct etiquette into our psyche. The rapid advances in technology and entertainment means there is no established etiquette guidebook. With no hereditary code to draw on, we have no option but to take the manners we have learnt in the home and try to apply them to the public sphere. And that's why the question of modern manners drives us to the brink of despair and frustration. Other people refuse to play ball. It's not us. It's them. It's not me – it's YOU. So, in this chapter, I am going to lay out some of the principle thorns in our collective side and then propose suitable, contemporary remedies.

So, let's start with communication and transport. First up – what are the ground rules on receiving or making a call on a train?

Well, I think we should begin by being honest. The real reason we get annoyed by people talking on their phones is not because of the noise levels, not because our delicate little ears can't handle the volume – it's because we simply can't hear the other side of the conversation. It's frustrating beyond measure to hear a mere 50 per cent of the discourse as it leaves us with so many unanswered questions. Why did Cheryl leave the party early? What are you going to have to tell Stuart in private before the board meeting tomorrow? What exactly has your wife promised to do for you in return for that trip to the Seychelles? The boozy bellowings of commuters would be infinitely more tolerable, even enjoyable, if we could learn more about the twonk they're chatting with.

The only indication for correct phone etiquette on public transport comes in the form of The Quiet Carriage. For those not familiar with The Quiet Carriage, it's business as usual, except people cup their hands over their mouth when they holler down their mobile phones.

What has been, laudably I should add, designed as an oasis of calm in a sea of noise pollution has turned out to be nothing more than a breeding ground of stress and resentment, where even the slightest breech of the decibel threshold can raise a hackle.

The first rule of The Quiet Carriage is: Don't Talk About The Quiet Carriage. The second rule of The Quiet Carriage is: Don't Talk IN The Quiet Carriage. This coach is populated by the Ear Police, those inveterate shh-monkeys who, in happier times, would be populating libraries. Now libraries are being closed left, right and LibDem – these silence-seekers have nowhere left in their search for total silence, other than the coaches of public transport. Heaven help you if you get caught by a member of the Ear Police. First, they will begin by tutting (anything more vociferous than that would be a direct contravention of The Quiet Carriage). Next comes the exaggerated eye-rolling and head-shaking – you know the kind of passive-aggressive play I'm referring to. It's a pressure cooker of stress which could erupt at any minute in any place, except in the very one that created it. Here's an idea for all those guilty of passive-aggressive harrumphing – if someone is annoying you, why not go up to them and calmly and politely tell them so. Watching them through the back of a teaspoon and occasionally sighing in a dramatic fashion simply isn't going to cut it.

Is it the end of days if someone speaks in The Quiet Carriage? I say no. The Ear Police say a resounding YES. They claim that if you allow the breaking of one trifling rule it creates a precedent – and then what are we left with? Anarchy! The Fall of Nations! That's what precipitated the collapse of the Roman Empire, some senator having a barney with his concubine below a sign which read: "TACETE!"

But what are the rules governing eating on public transport? The system as it stands is desperately inadequate. Currently you can either sit in standard class and enjoy the taste of someone's chips by osmosis or, for £15, upgrade to first class, where you get a better class of strep throat and the smell of your fellow passenger's dinner is less McDonald's and more Gourmet Burger Kitchen.

While I'm on the subject of food, let me reiterate a golden rule: never vomit on a Tube train. In fact, never vomit near a Tube train. It is simply the worst thing you can do. Imagine projectile barfing in the Large Hadron Collider and there you have it. It's a perfect storm down there in the Underground – everyone is in the blast radius. I know this to my cost. One evening, at Tottenham Court Road Tube, I got off a westbound Central Line train. At that moment, a woman vomited on the eastbound platform and an oncoming eastbound train pulled in. Even as I say this, I'm aware it sounds like a maths puzzle. Anyhow, the drag, or the wind resistance, or whatever, meant that her puke travelled down the interconnecting corridor and SPLAT into my hair.

It was shortly after that I got heavily into buses. After all, as Lord Buddha said (and he knew an awful lot about metropolitan travel): "It is better to travel well than arrive."

Next, is it ever acceptable to ask someone to stop talking on the mobile when it's disturbing your peace?

Yes. If that person is driving the bus or train that you happen to be a passenger on. There is nothing more disconcerting than a driver bellowing "WASSSSUP" down his iPhone while negotiating a hairpin bend. I once saw a TfL employee downloading a free fart app while manning the barriers. It's disrespectful – plain and simple.

Is there subject matter you should never discuss publicly while on the phone?

Well, I would recommend not revealing your PIN and/or bank account details – unless I am on the train with you and have a pen and paper to hand. I would also not discuss, in any detail, the results of your recent proctology examination. (It doesn't matter whether I am on the train with a notepad for this one.)

Is it ever acceptable to use a mobile in the cinema?

I think using your mobile IS acceptable if the film in question is one of the following:

Pearl Harbor

Jack and Jill

Highlander II: The Quickening

Jack and Jill (in case your eyes skipped over it first time. I do think it something of a public duty to warn people about this particular cinematic crock).

If you were in the movie theatre during any one of those shows, I would deem it highly acceptable to make a call. Actually, more than acceptable – I would consider it your duty. So much so I would be happy to provide the names and digits of the studio executives who commissioned such awful claptrap. I have *Jack and Jill* star Adam Sandler on speed dial.

However, if the film is a good one, then NO, absolutely not. Again, this is entirely down to personal taste. By NO, of course I mean: if it is something I might like. If you see me in the cinema and it's an intense indy film from Croatia or an action blockbuster or some sentimental pap about dogs then SHUT UP, I am enjoying myself. If it's a rom-com staring Jennifer Aniston, chat away – I know I will be.

Is it only talking that's unacceptable when you're watching a film or is the constant texting with the flashing phone light just as disturbing?

Now we're showing our age. Who's to say that teenagers today don't need the comforting blue glow of a smartphone backlight in the same way that Linus in the *Charlie Brown* cartoons needed his comfort blanket, or I needed my Hello Kitty nunchucks and My Little Pony throwing stars.

How much of your life should you expose on Facebook, Twitter and YouTube?

I'm a keen user of Twitter. By keen, I mean I spend 21 hours a day logged on. I do pause for the occasional tea break, which crucially means I'm keen, but not FANATICAL. I like nothing more than to be kept abreast of what strangers are having for their dinner (surely a hastily taken iPhoto of a plate of half-finished *huevos rancheros* is EXACTLY what the internet was invented for). I also need constant and immediate access to shots of kittens with a passing resemblance to Adolf Hitler and links to YouTube featuring impromptu boil lancings that have gone horribly, horribly wrong.

Social networking is not something that can be done by halves. You're in, or you're not. You are either permanently attached to your desk updating your status page – "It's raining... LOL", "Got to go to work now *sad face*", "I just ate a sandwich, ROFL" – or you're a lightweight, a part-timer. The internet has no use for part-timers. The way to tell if you're a proper, committed user is if, a couple of years into posting, you realise you haven't seen a human being, or breathed in fresh air, or touched anything living, or done anything interesting whatsoever to write about. That, my friends, is when you start owning cyberspace.

Is it ever acceptable to post a remark, a video of a friend or family member on any of the above without asking?

For me, it's all about the credit, baby. The truly great thing about Twitter is that it encourages the acknowledgment of sources. It's about crediting people via the RT or retweet. I know that might seem unnecessarily august – but 'fessing up where your material hails from is an important part of scholarship. In fact, it may well be the only bit of scholarship left to us in this day and age.

The downside of the "replicate and share" model of social media, however, does inevitably start to make us feel that there is no corner of our life which is private or sacrosanct. I once went to an awards do, had a few drinks and then had a few more drinks. Afterwards, I had a drink, which was so delicious I had another – which didn't sit right, so I had another three to wash the taste away. To cut a long story short, the evening ended with a rather charming young gentleman informing me of the silken texture of his testicles. I know, it's a scene straight out of Jane Austen. After making enquiries as to the veracity of this claim, this particular Mr Darcy unbuttoned his breeches and presented me with the items in question in order I might judge for myself. A split second later, a flash went off – a woman at the party had taken a photo of this charming scene – and before I could say "that's the end of my career" it was posted on Twitter. Did she ask my permission? No. Would I like it if she had? Yes. Would I have consented? Probably, but that's not the POINT. The point is, ask the guy whose ball-sack you have just sent viral.

Is it acceptable for potential or existing employers to check you out on any of the above? Many's the time I've skived off work, feigning Ebola, tennis elbow, rickets etc, only to be caught out by the fact I've posted a picture of myself drinking blue cocktails from a coconut shell. In Hawaii. Thankfully, one can always cry identity theft these days.

Now to a classic public transport dilemma – giving up your seat. Under what circumstances should my tush be moved? Well, this is a thorny issue. For instance, should you give up your seat to a man who is morbidly obese? Surely, him standing and improving his core strength by gentle stabilising motions as the train rocks to and fro is the only exercise he's going to get – and thus, you are doing him a favour. And what exactly is the etiquette for giving up your seat for a pregnant lady, when she is half my age. Does seniority or maternity confer a rested backside?

As lifespans increase, the age of retirement recedes onto the horizon and the definition of middle age widens, a new phenomenon is occurring. When you offer your seat to "an old person" they have started to say "no". Not only that, but they say that "no" in a horrified way, as if you've just swallowed the entire pack of their Werther's Originals without a by your leave. It's as if they are hissing: "Me? OLD? HOW DARE YOU?" Suddenly your act of altruism has been twisted into an act of hostility. People stare at you on the Tube, and the muttering starts. "Patronising," sneers one. "Gerontophobe," snarls another.

Is it acceptable to snog – and more – in public? Why do we as a nation recoil at public displays of affection? What's wrong with the odd ad-hoc snog? But that's as far as it should go. It's a fine line before snogging becomes dogging. Which is illegal, as I know to my cost.

Finally, I want to briefly discuss the delicate matter of fare evasion. Of course, not paying for your journey is a criminal offence, however, there is such a thing as an impolite and over-zealous revenue inspection. People object to astronomical rail fares because UK trains are, in essence, slow plague pits on wheels. Were the cast of *CSI* to enter a common or garden railway carriage and cast their ultra-violet scanner over a sample patch of wall, they would have a full-on seizure at the wealth of DNA material on offer. One particular journey I made from

Cornwall was notable for two reasons. First, from the off-set, we the passengers, were in real danger of being over-whelmed by the flood emanating from the toilets. The carpets in the carriage acted as blotting paper for the first 20 minutes, but thereafter the deluge was inescapable. Second, an hour into the journey, smoke started pour-ing from the train and we lurched to a halt. Time went by, and finally the customer service manager informed us that the train was kaput and that we would have to walk along the track to the next station and wait for a replacement bus. The doors were then opened and we were helped onto the gravel by a burly guard or two. So far, so good. What wasn't so good was that as they were bundling us down (and there were a good few pension-ers among our number who found the whole thing very stressful) the customer service manager thought it the perfect moment to stage a ticket inspection. The 80-year-old in front of me was given a fireman's lift, dumped on some loose chippings, pointed in the direction of the next station (a mile away) and then asked to provide proof of travel. There's a time and a place for the application of the law, and I can tell you it isn't dusk, trackside, some-where south-west of Liskeard.

Here are my suggestions for modern manners:

1. Mobile conversations SHOULD be allowed on trains, as long as they all take place on speaker-phone. No monologues allowed. Full transparency

or no call. Your choice.

2. Either there should be an Eating Carriage, in the same way there is a Quiet Carriage, or there should be fixed meal times on public transport. Breakfast from 7am until 9am, lunch from noon until 2pm and dinner from 6pm to 8pm. All meals consumed outside of these hours will be confiscated and given to the homeless.

3. All genitals should be micro-chipped, registered and licensed. Therefore, should someone wish to reproduce them, they have to get permission from the owner.

4. Image trading. Should a potential employer wish to look at a personal photo on your social networking site, they have to provide one in exchange. We ALL want to see Bill Gates at a stag do.

5. Everybody over the age of 70 MUST take a seat on public transport whether they want to or not. This age group will have designated seats, which can be distinguished by the rules of contract bridge which have been lovingly hand-embroidered on the arm rests by the local WI.

6. Equally, everybody who is more than six months pregnant MUST be made to stand. Their lives are about to become hell – they need to get used to it. It's not about them anymore. After all, nobody likes a selfish parent.

7. For acts of indecency there should be a strict time limit of 60 seconds. This will accommodate anything from a quick snog to a furtive grope, but should rule out intercourse. If it doesn't, you can guarantee the other person will be so disappointed they won't be returning for a repeat performance anyway.

8. I think it appropriate that free travel is given when it is technically possible to walk to your destination quicker than it is to use the public transportation system.

Sue Perkins is a comedian, broadcaster, writer and actor who appears on programmes including Have I Got News For You and Newsnight and BBC Radio 4. Her other work includes presenting the BBC Two hit The Great British Bake Off with Mel Giedroyc and food programmes with Giles Coren.

CHAPTER FOUR

I BLAME STEPHEN FRY
John Humphrys, on the death of respect

It was a warm summer's day and I was sitting in the office of my house in London gazing out of the window when I should have been bashing away at the keyboard. Walking down the street was a young girl – probably in her late teens – and approaching her from the other end was an old lady pulling her shopping trolley. As they drew nearer she glanced at the girl and then looked quickly away, clearly embarrassed. I wondered why and then I saw what the girl was wearing: a T-shirt with the words "F**k you" emblazoned across it. This happened in the closing months of the last century. Now spool back in time.

When my father was a similar age to the young girl, he took his fiancée to visit his aunt in her cottage in a small village in Somerset. They were about to sit down to Sunday lunch when the door burst open and the vicar – without so much as a "good morning" – marched in. The aunt leaped to her feet and dropped a little curtsey. The vicar, completely ignoring her guests, demanded: "Why were you not in church this morning, Mary Ellen?" She stammered something about her young nephew visiting, but the vicar turned on his heel and swept out with a brusque, "See that it doesn't happen again!" and was gone, leaving the door open behind him. Imagine his 21st century successor behaving like that today.

I suspect the four-letter word on the young girl's T-shirt might have been employed fairly liberally – if not by Great Aunt Mary Ellen then certainly by her young nephew. Quite right too, you will probably say, and I'd be tempted to agree with you. So what can have happened in the century spanning my two illustrations to have created such different attitudes? The first thing is that deference has died.

The dog collar that once accorded its wearer a certain automatic respect is now as likely to be treated with derision or simply ignored. And it's not just the church. It's the same with the other great institutions of State – the judiciary for instance. Judges were once seen as rather grand figures, remote from the common herd and unapproachable, but now they are more likely to be portrayed as out-of-touch toffs trying desperately (and not always successfully) to join the 21st century. And as for Parliament, what can one say? Anyone fancy a duck house on expenses?

The Monarchy is different. Maybe. We routinely tell opinion pollsters by a very large majority that we'd much prefer to keep the Crown than dump the Monarch in favour of a head of state we can vote for. But a little more persistent questioning suggests there may be an element here of Hilaire Belloc's admonition: "Always keep a-hold of Nurse; For fear of finding something worse." A more modern version used to be: "Prefer Maggie Thatcher would you?"

Yet, for all of her enormous popularity even our present Queen felt the sting of public disapproval when Princess Diana died and she failed to respond to the national mood in the way some newspapers deemed appropriate. And can anyone even recall the days when the *National Anthem* was played at the end of the last show-ing in the cinema and we all stood respectfully rather than race off to the nearest exit? As a nation we might still come over all soppy when a future King walks his pretty young bride down the aisle, but it's likely to be the soap opera aspect that drives the emotion rather more than any special reverence for Monarchy.

It's certainly true that the Queen is one of the most respected people in the land – but for much the same reason, perhaps, that we respect someone like David Attenborough. It's because of the dignity and dedication she personally has shown over the years at least as much as the institution that she represents. The nation is, after all, perfectly capable of eviscerating other senior Royals if we think they've overstepped the mark, behaved stupidly or taken us for granted.

As with the institutions, so it is with the professions. Now that we can Google our medical symptoms we no longer treat "the doctor" with reverence. The inverted commas vanished a while ago. We know doctors make mistakes and we expect them to be held to account for it when they do. Nor do we automatically defer to teachers – even head teachers – or police officers. We applaud them if they do a good job but we don't automatically assume that they will. On the contrary: we tend to err on the side of scepticism rather than instinctive approval.

When did you last see the tabloid press referring to nurses as "angels"? It used to be almost obligatory. Not any longer. There have been too many stories about too many nurses treating patients – especially older people – disgracefully. By contrast, there is no sign of "hero" being dropped when the tabloids write about soldiers in Afghanistan. If people risk their lives in the service of their country they are deemed to have earned our respect almost without qualification. Hard to argue with that. It is the unthinking, reflexive deference that has gone and the only people who might lament its passing are those who once benefited from it.

Respect is something else again. And here's where the teenage girl with the offensive T-shirt and the vicar with his even more offensive attitude have something in common. Neither of them showed respect. The girl was oblivious to the feelings of the old lady and the vicar treated my great aunt with contempt.

Deference was always different from respect because

it worked in only one direction. The absurdity of it was perfectly illustrated in that timeless sketch on BBC One in which the patrician John Cleese looked down on the middle-class Ronnie Barker and the poor little working-class Ronnie Corbett looked up to both of them. It was first shown in *The Frost Report* in 1966, a decade that delivered a hefty punch in the nose to the notion that people should be judged by their station in life rather than the way they lived their lives.

Deference was divisive: it fractured society. Respect is cohesive: it is part of the glue that binds us together. And I don't mean respect for our elders and "betters": I mean respect for each other. This is a crucial distinction, so let's give you another illustration.

The scene is a packed Underground train heading for the West End of London on a Saturday evening. A middle-aged woman – smartly dressed and carrying a book in one hand and a carrier bag in the other – squeezes into the seat next to me. She opens the bag and starts to remove its contents which she places very carefully on her lap: three plastic containers and a pair of chopsticks. She takes the lid off the first container and, using her chopsticks with skill and delicacy, starts to tuck into its contents. Then the next and then the next. In the time it takes to travel half a dozen stops she has polished off a three-course meal. I was half expecting her to summon a waiter and ask for the bill.

The food looked good but the smell was overpowering in that crammed, stuffy carriage. I noticed several of the other passengers wrinkling their noses in distaste but she, clearly, was entirely oblivious to us all. So I did what any red-blooded Welshman would do and confronted her.

"Madam!" I roared in my best Somerset vicar voice. "If I wanted to be surrounded by the smell of chop suey I would visit a Chinese restaurant. But I do not. Instead I wish to travel on this train without my nostrils being assailed so disgustingly. Kindly have some consideration for others!"

My fellow passengers rose as one to applaud and the woman, eyes downcast, tucked her chopsticks back in her bag and slunk off the train at the next station. I wish.

Of course, I did nothing of the sort. I just sat and suffered in silence, along with everyone else. Well, you never know do you? She might have exploded in anger and rammed a chopstick in my ear and the other passengers would, of course, have looked the other way. That's what we tend to do, isn't it?

Now let's not pretend that one selfish woman eating her dinner on a Tube train heralds the end of civilisation as we know it. But there is an awful lot of it about. Every time I have told that story I've been trumped by someone else with a worse one – though occasionally there is a happy ending. My colleague Jim Naughtie told me a classic mobile phone horror story.

The villain was a lawyer who destroyed the peace of her fellow passengers on a long train journey by end-lessly conducting various business transactions over her phone, bellowing into it so loudly it was impossible for everyone in the carriage not to listen. And then one of the passengers (Jim insists it wasn't him) sent her a text. It read something like: "As a result of being forced to listen to your conversation for the past two hours I now know a great deal about your private and professional life, including your name, phone number and credit card details. I have noted them down and rest assured I shall make good use of them if you do not shut up."

She went berserk, charging up and down the carriage demanding to know who had texted her. And the won-derful, glorious life-enhancing outcome was that not only did no one own up, but everyone told her to shut up and sit down. Oh, to have been there.

But, of course, it doesn't often work out like that. The more prosaic and deeply sad reality is that our public space is no longer protected from the bores and buffoons who have scant respect for anyone else's privacy. Until relatively recently they tended to be yobbish young men and (occasionally) women, who would stuff their faces with stinky hamburgers and generally behave loutishly. Now it is as likely to be the sort of people who would once have been regarded as their social superiors.

I made a series of reports for the *Today* programme as

part of our general election campaign coverage in 2010 to see how Britain had changed under the last government. For one I went back to my hometown of Cardiff. I was told I would be shocked by the scenes on Friday and Saturday nights. I was. The place had become a war zone, a no-go area for anyone wanting a pleasant evening out on the town. The police admitted to me that they had effectively handed the city centre over to the drunks. They simply closed off the main streets to traffic, parked plenty of police vans and ambulances in the middle of them for when serious trouble broke out (not IF but WHEN) and left them to it.

That was more or less what I had been warned to expect. What surprised me was how many of the drunks were not youngsters behaving badly the way they do when they've had a few too many, but groups of men and women in their thirties and forties – doctors, nurses, teachers, lawyers – who had gone out for the evening with the sole purpose of getting drunk. One group of women were celebrating their friend's 35th birthday by getting as many men as possible to stick their tongues down her throat. These were what we might have described in another time and another place as educated, middle-class women. I refused the invitation, but I was in a pretty small minority.

Vulgar but harmless fun, maybe, though not so harmless for the young police officer showing me round, who tried to separate a group of men and women when the inevitable fight broke out (the first of many) and was himself quite badly hurt when they turned on him. I asked his senior officer what had happened to respect for the law. He shrugged. He was as baffled as I.

You might argue that if we don't want to get involved in drunken brawls on a Friday or Saturday night the answer is simple: stay away. But why should we? Why should public spaces be denied to those of us who don't like watching people get roaring drunk, pick fights, urinate in the gutter and all the rest of it? If we are prepared to cede the town centre on Friday and Saturday nights to the drunks, where do we draw the line?

Swearing – loud and aggressive swearing – is virtually inescapable in public places. As someone who has been known to utter the odd expletive himself, I can hardly claim to be shocked by swearing but I don't want my youngest child or the old lady in my street to be subjected to it if she'd prefer not to be. And no, it was not always so. My father was a hard-working, hard-drinking man who was a labourer in a steel mill for several years and I suppose it's just possible that his vocabulary might have strayed beyond "bother!" or even "drat!" if a red hot ingot fell on his foot. I have no doubt that the language he used in the mill or on the docks was every bit as colourful as any other steelworker or docker but he never, ever, swore at home or in public.

That might puzzle the great Stephen Fry because he says swearing is a really important part of life and that people who think like my father are "mad, silly and prissy". I'll spare you some of his other thoughts on the subject, this being a respectable publication, and merely observe that he is talking utter tosh. National treasure with a brain the size of Jupiter he undoubtedly is, but I'd love to see him explain his barmy thoughts on swearing to the teacher struggling hopelessly with a class of children who can see no reason why they shouldn't use the f-word in every other sentence.

After all, they hear it everywhere they go, don't they? Doesn't do any harm, does it? Nobody would make a fuss if they said "fluck", would they? These are just silly old conventions. Something we find offensive today will probably be entirely acceptable tomorrow. True, true... but all this misses the point entirely. Youngsters who swear loudly in front of a teacher in a classroom or a policeman on the street are usually well aware that it is causing offence. That's why they do it.

Of course it's true that language must evolve endlessly. That's the glorious thing about it. It's also true that there's no logic in regarding the arrangement of a group of letters in one way as perfectly benign and in another way as hugely offensive, but that also misses the point. It's not a matter of logic. It is the meaning attributed to the word and the intention behind their use that matters. The clothing firm French Connection UK garnered millions of pounds of free publicity in 1997 by discovering the acronym of its initials and plastering them over T-shirts. Their expressions of injured innocence when it was suggested that they were deliberately setting out to create controversy were a joy to behold. An official statement from the tooth fairy would have carried more conviction.

So let's not patronise young people who swear aggressively in public by suggesting they're too stupid to know what they're doing. The word "dissing" was invented on the street and to "diss" someone else can be dangerous. Too many young people have been attacked – sometimes fatally – because they were deemed not to have shown respect. Well, exercising linguistic restraint is one way of showing respect.

I spent a year making a BBC Two documentary about the state of education in Britain's schools and if I took away one single message it was that the schools where the teachers were respected were the schools that delivered the best education. And "respect" meant the children did not swear in their presence. Ever.

The Police Federation was mightily upset with a High Court judge, Mr Justice Bean, when he quashed the conviction in a magistrates' court of a young man who had been fined £50 for repeatedly swearing at two police officers. The swear words, he said, were heard "all too frequently" by police officers on duty and so were unlikely to have caused them "harassment, alarm or distress". No doubt he's right about that. I struggle with the image of a tough policeman dissolving into tears because he has heard a young tough telling someone to "eff off" on the street. But I have no difficulty imagining the timid old lady in my street being visibly alarmed and distressed. Not that I need to imagine it: most of us have seen it happen all too often. Maybe future generations of little old ladies will become inured to it in the same way as today's hard-nosed police officers and they'll tell the yobs to "eff off" in return, but I don't relish the thought. I'd prefer my children and grandchildren to grow up in a society where there's a bit of mutual respect.

There are some signs that the worm is beginning to turn. The more right-wing newspapers such as the *Daily Mail* have been warning about what is happening to society for a very long time. That's what is expected of them. But not so that standard bearer of the liberal left, *The Guardian*. It was, I think, the first national newspaper to print four-letter words (even the rudest) without asterisks and is the polar opposite of the *Daily Mail* in almost every respect. But towards the end of 2011 it devoted five pages to what it described as the "ugly mood" in the air in Britain under the headline, "Angry Britain: why are we becoming so intolerant?". The writer Hugh Muir recalled the 1973 Hollywood film, *The Crazies*, with its absurd plot in which a god-fearing, strait-laced town goes haywire when somebody puts something nasty in the drinking water. Suddenly, decent folk turn very nasty indeed. The thin veneer of civilisation disintegrates.

Britain in December 2011 feels a bit like that place, wrote Muir. There is "an element of devil-may-care to the way we treat each other. You see it on the streets, on public transport, in the supermarket queues, read it on the internet threads".

Professor Cary Cooper, pro vice chancellor of Lancaster University, was quoted as saying what we are witnessing is "an exercise in civic frustration". At the root of it is the hard times we are going through. "People feel financial insecurity, job insecurity... They feel social insecurity and project it on to other people," he said. Well, maybe there's something in that, but it sounds like a pretty poor excuse to me, rather than an explanation. I'm old enough to remember the austerity years immediately after the last war when hardship was on a different scale altogether, when the poorest kids would pick up an apple core if you dropped it in the street and their homes would have packing cases for furniture and newspaper for a table cloth and they shivered in the winter because they did not own a decent coat.

At this point you might be expecting me to go off on a nostalgic riff about how we might have been poor in those days but at least we behaved with respect and we cared for each other, shared whatever we had and bore

our poverty with a brave smile. If only. There is nothing noble or life-enhancing about that kind of poverty.
It is oppressive and degrading and utterly soul-sapping.
If people did not get as angry in public then as they do
today I suspect it was partly because the energy of the
poorest went into the business of surviving – the endless effort to keep their children reasonably housed and
clothed and fed. No one could possibly hanker after those
days – even if we did behave in a more civilised way
towards each other.

And in any case, nostalgia never solved anything. Better, perhaps, to look at the ways in which society has
changed. One is that we have succumbed to the strange
affliction of emotional incontinence. Its symptoms have
been appearing for the past couple of decades – most obviously the bizarre overreaction to the death of Princess
Diana in 1997 and the birth of *Big Brother*. With its insa-
tiable appetite for sad souls desperate to become famous
by humiliating themselves in front of the cameras, reality television gave a licence to the kind of behaviour in
public that would once have been regarded as shaming.
Compare the first programmes, which offered some genuine insight into human interaction, with the freak show
it was to become. The notion that restraint might ever be
desirable was put to the torch. The lasting effect is that
no light entertainment television show is complete today
without somebody – ideally lots of people – shrieking or

weeping, or preferably both.

Restraint tends to be sneered at and the stiff upper lip has become a bit of a joke. If that's the case, perhaps somebody should tell those brave men and women who fought in World War Two and who we still hear occasionally speaking with such dignity and, usually, reluctance about what happened to them. As I write, I've just been listening to a woman describing on BBC Radio 4 how her mother kept her alive in the Burmese jungle when they were being chased by Japanese soldiers. She was the only child in her group to survive. Her mother's behaviour was heroic. She herself never spoke of it.

There is, it seems to me, a clear line connecting restraint and respect and the loss of both have led to that "ugly mood" described so well in *The Guardian*. The yobs who deface war memorials and dishonour the war dead are at the extreme end of the scale with plenty of space left for the weekend drunks and the loud-mouthed, foul-mouthed swearers and the boorish passengers and the selfish drivers and all the others who make life miserable for people trying to go about their daily business in the public space.

So the solution? Simple. Rehabilitate the concept of respect. Call it restraint if you prefer or good manners or consideration for others or any one of a dozen other things. It really doesn't matter what you call it because we all know it when we see it.

And how do you do that? Ah, that's where it gets

tricky. We could start with the schools and move into the television boardrooms and then, if all else fails, recruit Stephen Fry. I'll bet he has a few ideas on the subject.

John Humphrys is known for his combative interviewing style on BBC Radio 4's Today programme, which he has presented since 1987. He has been a journalist for the BBC since 1966, presenting and reporting on news at home and abroad. John also presents Mastermind on BBC Two.

CHAPTER FIVE

I BLAME THE PARENTS
Rachel Johnson, on children's behaviour

"The toughest job in the world is not being President. It's being a parent." – Bill Clinton

This quote I've kicked off with? Well, I'M SORRY but it makes me want to emit a wordless, silent howl. I much prefer this lapidary lamentation that mirrors my mood so much better.

"Times are bad. Children no longer obey their parents and everyone is writing a book." Yes, Marcus Tullius Cicero got it about right two thousand years ago. Everyone thinks that the next generation is more feckless, irresponsible, and disrespectful than the last, as the Latin motto *"O tempora! O mores!"* never fails to remind us.

In that sense our generation is no different. Which means there is cold comfort in the knowledge that even in Augustan Rome, disapproving matrons in togas tut-tutted at the way children got down from the *triclinium* without asking, were rowdy during the Feast of Lupercalia, were rude to slaves, and so on.

In many ways, nothing changes. We love our children. We want them to grow up to be competent, decent human beings fit for adult purpose. These are the main things, and in these main things, we have – I think we are all agreed – done not too badly. Our children – and I think I am permitted to generalise here – are not serial axe-murderers and psychopathic kitten-drowners. And although feted interior designer Nicky Haslam says "loving your parents" is rather common (as, in his world, are celebrity chefs, bottled water and swans) our children do seem to make an effort on special occasions anyway to repay the enormous investment of time, energy, money and emotion we have poured into them. Children are programmed to please, to be loved, and to love us back. Thank God.

So what we are here to examine chiefly is not the children. They are examined enough as it is, from Sats via Gove-levels all the way to finals. No, the kids are all right. Where we should peer in this chapter is under the stone, at the dark, damp place where pale worms feebly wriggle, for this is the condition of the modern parent, in order to try to determine where we – and I include myself – have gone so terribly wrong.

For my chosen experts – whom we shall hear from in a bit – agree we have. Listen to what English teacher David McCullough told high school leavers in Wellesley, Massachusetts, in June 2012 in his commencement address, entitled You're Not Special, and weep with appalled recognition.

"Yes, you've been pampered, cosseted, doted upon,

helmeted, bubble-wrapped. Yes, capable adults with other things to do have held you, kissed you, fed you, wiped your mouth, wiped your bottom, trained you, taught you, tutored you, coached you, listened to you, counselled you, encouraged you, consoled you and encouraged you again. You've been nudged, cajoled, wheedled and implored. You've been feted and fawned over and called Sweetie Pie. Yes, you have. And, certainly, we've been to your games, your plays, your recitals, your science fairs. Absolutely, smiles ignite when you walk into a room, and hundreds gasp with delight at your every tweet."

But before we come to the wretchedly indulgent state of parenting that McCullough has so amply illustrated above, I suppose I had better set out my stall. Inevitably, when one becomes a parent, one can't help revisiting one's own childhood, in order to make invidious comparisons between then and now. The two main differences I find between my childhood and my parenthood are these:

1. When I was little, we were given no choices – about what we ate, wore, did, when we went to school, bed etc. I could choose only what to read.
2. There was not so much stuff (a lot of my son's 15-year-old friends have iPods, iPads, MacBooks, unlimited access to their parents' credit cards, PayPal, eBay, and iTunes accounts, and not just an iPhone but a BlackBerry too). We made our

own fun, rather than bought it in the Westfield shopping centre.

My parents provided us with the essentials then got on with their own lives. Which makes me realise they were brilliant, not because of what they did, but more what they didn't do. So we were fed, we were clothed, we were loved, and we had all the books we could read and the best education that money could buy. But there was not the life of plenty, the expectation of having every wish granted that there is now, and that is the best thing my parents could ever give us.

I remember only once going to a restaurant in the UK (if memory serves it was a Happy Eater on the A303) and being told we could have the spag bol, from the children's menu. We had a TV, but as we lived in Belgium there was nothing to watch apart from two American sitcoms that came on once a week.

We were so poor that when we went to England (for holidays on Exmoor mainly spent "wooding" for winter fuel on rainswept hillsides) my father would invariably book the cheap overnight ferry crossings. He would never shell out for a cabin, despite a 1am departure.

Instead, Dada – having formally slipped into some striped flannel PJs for the occasion – would tell us to go to sleep in the back of the Opel Kadett, parked with the handbrake on in the lower deck for the duration, where we would either pass out from diesel fumes, or the reek of each other's vomit.

We never had friends round for "play dates" either. Keeping children busy and happy was not a constant parental priority. If we were bored, that was our own fault. In fact, there was nothing to do for weeks on end except read on our beds. Occasionally my mother would shout up the stairs: "Stop reading!" Imagine that now, when children are on their laptops in their rooms, looking at – I don't want to imagine.

Once, and only once, my older brother had a friend round who, as soon as I said hello, punched me in the head. This was water off a duck's back. Not only did I have three brothers to fight, my father and my mother both believed enthusiastically in corporal punishment. My mother once broke a large stick over my legs after Boris and I had spent a happy and, we felt, productive morning carefully filling every single Wellington boot in the passage to the brim with water. I bear neither parent any ill feeling for beating me. I would have done the same.

My mother tells the story of how, when we lived in Washington DC, she was racing to meet my father with Boris aged four and me, three. As crowds surged and pressed behind us to cross the four-lane highway, I refused to cross Pennsylvania Avenue. In the end, she had to pick me up by my hair, at which point a woman stormed: "You don't deserve to have that little girl."

But she did deserve me; rather, I didn't deserve her. One of her most revealing relics of the tribal Johnson childhood (she has also kept our first hair clippings and baby teeth, and all our exercise books for the year she home-schooled us, one of my happiest childhood memories) is a note composed by Boris and signed by all four of us children saying: "Dear Mama WE are SORY that we were SO BAD today."

As for school – well, reports were read, but not dwelt upon, as they were also not my parents' business, but ours. As for parental involvement – well, all I can tell you is that my father's proudest boast as a parent is not that all his children went to Oxbridge but that he never, once, attended a parent-teacher meeting at any one of our various schools.

When I was ten and Boris 11, my mother would drop us at the Gare du Nord in Brussels with our school trunks, hand over a few *francs* for *frites* on the ferry, and then get back to the much more interesting business of painting or seeing her psychiatrist, a tall gingery man called Dr Mols. We would get on a train to Ostend. We would then get on the ferry to Dover. At Dover, we would get the train to London Victoria, where we would interchange for Forest Row. There were very few trains to Forest Row then (there are even fewer trains to Forest Row now) so Boris and I would kill time in the Cartoon Cinema, where paedophiles in brown macs were waiting for little lost schoolchildren just like us to wander in, so they could offer us "sweets". Then we would get our trunks on the stopping train to Forest Row. It would take all day, and was problem-free until the time when we did the journey in reverse during the Cold War of the Seventies and managed, as soon as we had made landfall in the Continent, to get on the train to Moscow instead.

The point is, I suppose, my parents never worried even when, one half-term, I was an unaccompanied minor and the British Caledonian airline stewardess supposed to be looking after me forgot to put me on the plane and I had to spend the week in the Trusthouse Forte at Gatwick airport on my own instead.

As I say, it never did me any harm, but still, I can't repeat this sensible regime of character-building, toughening, anecdote-forging benign neglect for my own children... and nor, it appears, can anyone else. Now examples of wet parenting abound.

Mary Killen, author of *How The Queen Can Make You Happy*, agony aunt for *The Spectator*, and mother of two daughters, admits she is a classic example of a wet modern parent. Especially when it came to the gap year of her older daughter, Freya. For this important period for the young adult about to take wing into the world, Mary paid an older male student to accompany Freya, 19.

"Yes, I did pay Karl to go on her gap year with her," Mary said, by way of explanation. "You see, Freya had grown up in a tiny Wiltshire village, where all the men were nice, or at least not active sex offenders. I knew that if I didn't hire a male chaperone, she would be raped and beheaded on her first day, and weeks later her body would be found in the bottom of a ravine."

"But she was going to Italy!" I shrilled. "It's not exactly darkest Peru! I still don't understand why you couldn't let her go to Tuscany on her own."

"The truth is, I had to pay someone not just to fend off rapists," Mary confessed at my query, "but also to be the person who swept up all the passports, purses, airline tickets, keys and so on that Freya litters on tables when she leaves restaurants."

Killen is, of course, *sui generis*, but she is representative of a world where a manic Chinese mom calls herself a Tiger Mother and writes a bestselling book about how to produce straight-A violin-playing tennis-champ superkids, and where pushy, anxious, helicopter parents hover over every school. A friend reports that when her son was due to visit the Brecon Beacons on a school camping trip in the summer term, something the entire year was going on, three mothers pulled out their huge teenage sons on the grounds that the weather forecast was "rainy". Parents are even meddling in universities, to the extent that dons are complaining of a traumatic level of parental over-involvement just at the exact moment that mummies and daddies are supposed to be letting go.

Parents now not only accompany their children to entrance days, they fill out their Ucas forms. They arrive laden with duck-down duvets at the start of freshers' week, and then, worst of all, don't proceed to leave.

In Bristol, mothers have been spending up to a week dossing down in the dorm with their daughters at university. This has led beleaguered dons to warn that students are becoming "infantilised" due to their parents' presence.

It was the complete opposite in my day. When I was on my gap year I called my father from Israel in September and told him I'd decided not to take up my place at Oxford. I announced I wanted to stay in Galilee with a handsome Israeli shepherd called Ehud. For ever. My father didn't miss a beat. "Great scheme!" he cried, astutely divining that if he approved the plan, I'd never carry it out.

Hillary Clinton was teased for producing a book about "doing kids" (as they say in the US) called *It Takes A Village*. But what she was pointing out (I say this authoritatively but I doubt that I, or anyone else, has ever read the volume) was that how you bring up your children is a collective effort with its own ripple effect. Do it well, and you spread the love, like in a Coca Cola advert. Do it badly, and you can poison the whole well.

This is why wet parenting is such a dreaded development. Not only does our coddling of our young fail to prepare them for leaving the nest, the rigours of employment, self-catering, London transport and earning a living in a recession, it doesn't even prepare them to do the most basic of household tasks. Having members of society who have only ever been feather-bedded, pampered, chauffeured from A to B, privately tutored, and had their bottoms wiped since birth is bad news for us all. We have bred a generation of spoilt, rude incompetents.

And this has happened, despite – or is it because of – the professionalisation of parenting. If you type the word "parenting" into Google, it returns 318 million results. If you put the words "parenting courses" into Google, it comes up with 23 million hits. Can you face hearing about what's available on Amazon? Well I'm afraid that at the click of the mouse you could order, in ascending order: 1,583 books on grandparents; 2,700 books on fatherhood; 6,085 books on motherhood; 30,487 books on pregnancy and childcare; and a whopping 49,648 on "raising children".

See what I mean? Parenting has become fetishised, state-subsidised, professionalised, even though anyone can (and frankly, does) have a baby, after which, they become parents.

In my lifetime, a common experience has undergone a terrifying transition. Becoming a mother or father is no longer something you just are. It is something you do, like becoming a vet. In fact, it's a whole separate full-time career, complete with training courses, parenting vouchers cashable at Boots, government guidelines and targets, and a host of academics, caring professionals – and websites and helplines – on hand 24/7/12/365 to guide you from what to expect when you're expecting, to dealing with boomerang kids when your twenty-somethings crawl back home.

And yet, as my chosen experts themselves admit, children's behaviour is worse than ever. "It's because two working parents don't just want to shout at their children in the short interval that's left between coming home from work and putting them to bed," says Mary Killen. "People nowadays are prepared to send their dogs for training, but won't do the same for their own offspring."

Victoria Mather, author of *Social Stereotypes*, agrees that parents these days do not mete out the cruelty necessary for kiddie-house training. "As a result, children come out of school ignorant, dependent, entitled and ill-mannered, a privilege for which parents tend to pay a great deal of money," she observes. "Not to mention, they have no concept of manners, or privacy. I've had godchildren open my fridge and cupboards, help themselves to my food and wear my clothes – and I might add that a text is NOT a thank you letter."

To conclude, all I can say is this: don't bring up your children with the crazy idea that they're special. You are making a rod for your own back. As David McCullough concluded in his commencement address: "The sweetest joys of life, then, come only with the recognition that you're not special. Because everyone is."

Our children may not be special but secretly, I think being a parent is pretty special. I've enjoyed bits of it, anyway. But the bald facts are that it's unpaid and you never get to retire. So may I suggest, instead, an alternative way forward to wet parenting that might better work for parents, children and society as a whole?

Herewith, then, my top ten tips for Unparenting and raising a generation of well-mannered, better-balanced children. How I wish I'd followed them all myself, gripped this earlier, and then my work would be done.

1. Do not do your children's homework for them.
2. Do not ask them whether they have done their homework.
3. Do not offer a menu of foods at any meal – it only encourages them to go *a la carte*.
4. Resist all guilt-making attempts by your child's school to manifest repeatedly in person on endless trips/special activity days/visiting speakers etc. But DO show up for sports, sports days and prize days.
5. Smile brightly when your child tells you that you were "the only mother in the whole year who didn't come".
6. React in exactly the same way to good exam results and poor exam results.

7. Do NOT offer your child prize money or other presents to pass exams or get into Eton. Effort recognised is its own reward.
8. Do not make a meal of school reports.
9. Encourage your children to do grunt jobs in the holidays so they know the value of money and how boring it is to earn it, starting out.
10. Ban smartphones during all meals. Make everyone switch them off (we think children are welded to theirs but parents are just as bad), which means you can't secretly read emails while your children are telling you the whole plot of the fifth Harry Potter. You actually have to listen.

Rachel Johnson is editor-in-chief of The Lady and the author of several novels and volumes of diaries including Notting Hell and The Mummy Diaries. Her new novel, Winter Games, is out now. She lives in London and Somerset with her husband and three teenage children.

HOW RUDE!

CHAPTER SIX

MEN ARE FROM EARTH... AND SO ARE WOMEN
Fi Glover, on the gender agenda

Let me introduce you to The Oblivions – a fabulous term coined by Cyd of Toronto in Canada as part of a discussion in a chatroom in her native country about the manners of young people. I do hope she knocked before entering. The Oblivions is the phrase she uses for those boys and girls who appear to view the world from behind a portcullis of nonchalance. They're the ones who, when you want to get on a packed Tube, stare straight through you. It's a mighty stare as well, saying more than, "Am I bovvered?" It says: "I don't care about you", and it says it in a thousand different ways. It says: "I won't pick up that piece of litter, I won't hold the door open for you, I'm not going to apologise for pushing past you and I'm certainly not going to say 'top of the morning' to you." The girls of Oblivion are ruder than the boys, and sometimes their androgyny makes simple identification an arduous task. They can give you a look that kills kindness at 20 paces. It's often accompanied by white strings of an iPod attached to the ears, and some kind of computerised device in the hand. Both those things close off their world. But only to us, not to them – to them those worlds are huge and free and more liberating than anything we (I'm 43) ever had at our disposal. But what price that freedom? What exactly have we lost and what has it been replaced by? That is what we have to ask if we want to consider the manners that lie between the sexes now.

If we believed the headlines then we'd think that young men aren't even sending flowers anymore, they're just texting pictures of what is in their pants. We'd think that the only thing girls are waiting for is an upgrade to a device that can carry BlackBerry messaging services. We'd think the gentle path we used to call courting has been lost forever – it's the weed-strewn Beeching railway track lying unused beside the super-highway of social-networking love. And it's true that now you can meet someone on a Monday, be LinkedIn by Tuesday, have read their entire back catalogue of tweets by Wednesday, and by the end of Thursday you'll be "friends" with all of their exes via Facebook. And if your new love doesn't respond to you immediately – oh, is that the sweet pain of anticipation? Or are they just not in a Wi-Fi zone?

It's easy to fear the unknown and that is what this great new world of technology is to all but a few. There are already tomes about how you shouldn't text your new lover back until three days have passed, and then you must never use a "smiley face". There are manuals about how to write your entry on an internet dating site, how to behave on your first real-life meeting, what your virtual world avatar might really say about you etc etc etc. But let's hold on to our white horses because I suspect that, as ever, love is a greater thing than the use of mobile communication punctuation. And I also know that this frontier generation doesn't want rules. Like The Oblivions of Socrates' time, it has been born with the feeling that it's making them up. And that's fine, because I'm pretty sure that deep down the bit that makes things work between men and women stays the same: the tiny bit of instinct that tells you when you are in safe hands. So when it comes to the manners of men versus women we need to get past The Oblivions (just give them a shove, they'll love that) and look at the smaller picture – not the broad brush-stroke of an insolent youth but the more complex background detail.

And this is why I would like to share with you my Speedo Rule. I once went out with a very nice man called Peter. He was kind, considerate, had a good job, we both found each other quite interesting and he had a tiny but welcoming flat in Putney. After a couple of dates I found myself there of a morning (I am sorry if you find that shocking – I was about 25 at the time). He'd gone to work and his wardrobe was open. So I looked in it, which I admit is not a particularly polite thing to do. But curiosity got the better of me and I suppose I sensed there may be something in there I needed to know about. And there was. Quite clearly displayed was a pair of sandals. Not any old sandals – open-toed, geography teacher, well worn, hairy-toed sandals. Now cast your mind back to the early Nineties and a time when sandals had not made it on to the ironic, pedicured feet of the festival-loving classes they have now. Peter's sandals shouted, "I'm not ironic!" at me. They were very much there to be used. And they freaked me out. Because in my naive mind they were a sign. A sign of what might happen in the wardrobe department further down the line. I was suddenly standing on the top of a slippery slope in the fashion stakes, because although you might start with a hygienic sandal on a hot day in summer, pretty soon they're being worn with socks "because they are so comfortable" and then they're being worn with nothing but a pair of Speedos and before you know it you're on an orienteering holiday in Austria with meditation in the evening and seriously considering adopting the vegan lifestyle on the outskirts of a north German town. So I ran for the hills. And the thing about the Speedo Rule is that it applies to manners too. It's all a great big sliding scale. And the man who lets a door slam in your face, who lets you struggle to the car under your own body weight of groceries, who is too busy to write a thank-you letter to your maiden aunt – even if the Pavlova is still stuck to his teeth – and who doesn't notice when anyone's glass needs cheering up... well, ladies, don't be surprised when he won't get up in the middle of the night to feed a hungry baby. Don't come whining to me when he doesn't notice you are down in the dumps over some career or friendship blip. God forbid you get ill! Would he put your needs above his own?

I know a man who yawned his way, quite openly, through the first line of his own wedding. That was a sign too. Ten years on he's rarely at home, always working, needs his own study although his kids clearly want a room of their own too. His wife is fed up. He is one of many examples where manners – and the lack of them – have been the thin end of the wedge. In order for someone to even have them in the first place, they must have had it drummed into them that other people's needs are as great, if not greater, than their own. And that is a message that runs all the way through life's stick of rock.

Now if you think I am just going to rant about men who no longer carry handkerchiefs, well, I am not. But until the think-like-a-man-for-an-hour (do not take with alcohol) pill becomes available, I am going to have to write from the perspective of a lady – because, er, I am one. And we don't come out of it all that well. I suspect that we want our cake – served delicately on a bone china plate – and then we want to eat it too with all the decorum usually reserved for a fried chicken hangover box.

In creating the Speedo Rule you can see that I have adopted the moral high ground while getting there by a dubious route. And you are right to note that Peter probably had a similar sliding scale called the Poke Your Nose In with which he clearly recognised that if I was going through his cupboards in my twenties, it would be his mobile phone records in my thirties and his bank statements by the time I was 40. I seem to recall little resistance when I announced my desire not to come to Putney again. Oh, and as we're passing that milestone of How To Chuck Someone, there is a well-mannered way to do that for both sexes. Always blame your own failings not theirs, leave with a firm hug but no kiss and find one thing to say that you'll miss about them (even if it is just their eyelashes) – and then run for the hills and don't come back. It doesn't matter if you are a boy or a girl – seize the day and all that.

So if the big things are so easy to advise on, what about all the smaller things? Why do manners seem to be a quaint detail of the tea towel of life to so many people? Are we in a 21st century quandary? Well, let's recognise a great big truth first. The basis on which modern manners are founded is that Men Are From Strong Place, Women Are From Weak Place. The holding open of the door, the standing up when a lady enters a room, even women retiring to the drawing room (actually so that they could go for a comfort break without drawing attention to themselves) – these are all based on the notion that women need to be taken care of more. At the height of mannered society – surely the Victorian era – the etiquette between men and women dominated their lives. Everything from the way you spoke to the way you ate to the way you looked to the way you breathed was one long, coded message saying: "Why did I have to be born now?" Most of it was designed to constrain. One manual chastises women for doing something so "insincere" as to dye their hair. It advises they should walk with feet gently turned outwards, they should never hurry. They should stay silent until spoken to in company. That overly poised look that is now so celebrated in period drama – and becomes more and more intriguing in literature as time passes – would have been a prison. I know sistaz, we ain't going back there are we? Or are we? The only modern manuals for women's manners I have found still nod to that same sense that there is a fairer sex. (I have read quite a few so you can go and do something more fulfilling with your time.) Some still have sections advising you on how to buy a nice gift for someone, how to dress a dinner table, one that still states you shouldn't wear diamonds or pearls in the morning. I don't know about you but I've got all the time in the world to pop home and change my jewellery. And all of this is just silliness. Should you wish to read about the real change in women's lives your shelves can be groaning with the best from Gloria Steinem, Germaine Greer, Naomi Wolf et al. But the point is that women have found it hard to know what to replace that demure sense of mannered behaviour with, especially if they find themselves in more traditional male roles of power. It's interesting to note that the modern best-selling manuals for boys advocate a return to danger, not the embracing of more domesticity – even though there is still quite a lot of washing up to be done.

So if it's equality that we want, then where does etiquette fit in. Does she really need a door opened for her? Does he need to have his food served first? Can she ask him to marry her? Does she have to get down on bended knee for that? If it's the lady who is going to pick up the tab at dinner then should it be the lady who chooses the wine? Is it patronising for the liberated girl to be gently guided into a restaurant by a foot soldier of love, hand in the small of her back? Although it's quite nice to arrive in a room first does that actually, within seconds, negate the strides we have made in seeking equal pay, the ability to buy a house of our own, to have children or not have children and still have a life outside the home? Take the received wisdom that the first person you should serve at a supper table is the lady who has come the furthest to be there – on account of how she might swoon with hunger if you don't. Well what happens if the person who has made the most effort and is the most hungry is actually not Priscilla from Penge – successful company director and former member of the K2 tax scheme – but Kenneth from Clacton, feeble old misanthrope? Who gets the turkey first? Should that really have anything to do with gender?

And if it's the bloke who stays at home to raise the family and take care of the house, is it him who writes the thank-you letters and pops round with a cake when someone is having a hard time in the street?

I could pose a thousand questions to you and I bet that you would have a different answer to each. You could think through all of your friends and family and find someone who bucks the trend in at least five categories. Because here and now there is no hard and fast rule, is there? It just depends doesn't it? It depends on – and wait for it because I'm going to offer you another 21st century concept here, up there with the Speedos – it depends on code-shifting. If you haven't yet come across this marvellous phrase then can I formally introduce it to you? It's the ability to be a lot of different things to different people, and the ability to do that without feeling that your brain has gone bonkers, and you are being a total fraud.

In terms of manners, I can give you an example. I have an important friend (only one mind you) who sits on the board of many a big company. She has to stop herself serving tea in the boardroom when it arrives because, she rightly points out, as the only woman there it's sometimes assumed that it's her role – and it is jolly well not. It's not that she doesn't have impeccable manners; she does. She is one of the most polite people I know. She writes a great thank-you card and is a dignified and gracious woman. But of course she shouldn't pour the tea in a board meeting if she doesn't want to. One of the men (and the rest of them are all men) could put everyone at their ease, not leave my friend in an awkward place and just as easily hand round the drinks without losing any sense of power in the process. He'd be code-shifting, just like I would be if I offered to pick up the tab in a restaurant when taking a junior male colleague out to lunch. And now we are getting to the nub of it. We must adapt our sexual manners according to the situation we are in, without fearing that we demean ourselves in any way, on either side. There is no manual anymore. Just think how a modern-day Elizabeth Bennet would behave if her life were updated and she and Darcy were running Pemberley as an upmarket rehabilitation clinic or posh B&B. Not for her the downward gaze and faux demure pose, she'd be striding about with a clipboard looking people in the eye and getting things done. And it wouldn't mean that Darcy would be simpering away in a corner folding napkins. We don't have to swap our manners in order to get along.

But all of this is not to say that there shouldn't remain a healthy gap between the sexes. Androgyny is the unwelcome guest at the equality disco because if we all try to be the same, what exactly do we gain? If we are all holding open doors for each other at the same time, will anyone actually get where they need to be? Modern, strong and confident men and women are both capable of doing the Christmas cards, asking after each other's well-being and making a small hot drink when necessary. We don't have to do it all at the same time.

So I'm afraid it is just code-shifting and the Speedo Rule from me. The tiny things will tell you more about the big things than the big things ever could.

In the early days of our relationship, Rick spotted my table was wobbling (this is not a euphemism, behave yourselves). "I'll fix that for you," he said. And no sooner had I found him the tool kit than he'd turned the table over on the kitchen floor and got to work on the problem corner. "That bracket's not true," he said. And as in the great line in *Jerry Maguire* when she says: "You had me at 'hello'," he had me at "bracket".* It was quite a manly thing to do, in many senses it was old-fashioned, but it was also quite modern because it was my house, my kitchen table, my tool kit, he may well have just made the tea, I might have picked up the tab at lunch, I probably changed the oil in his car...

See what I mean? You can code-shift your way through the rest of your life, donning the power shoulders, drawing in the domestic, wearing the pants, putting on the smileys – whatever it is you would like to do. But between boys and girls – or boys and boys and girls and girls – good manners will always remain the same. They are sparkles of kindness in the grey concrete of life. Enjoy them wherever you find them.

*Of course, the timeline isn't quite true – I had already checked his cupboard and yes, appropriate footwear and swimwear was in there.

Fi Glover is a multi award-winning radio presenter and writer. She presented Saturday Live on BBC Radio 4 for five years, leaving in 2011 and now presents The Listening Project for BBC Radio. Fi is also a columnist for Waitrose Weekend. She lives in London with her partner, Rick, and two children.

CHAPTER SEVEN

NO MORE HEROES ANYMORE
Quentin Letts, on setting an example

In 1977 The Stranglers produced a punky album called *No More Heroes* which had a cover featuring a coffin with roses and rats' tails. "Whatever happened to all the heroes?" ran the lyrics. "All the Shakespearoes?" Thirty-five years on, the matter is, if anything, more urgent. What, indeed, has happened to the leaders of our country? A land without heroes is a land without ideals. Their absence may help to explain our drift, our cultural insecurity, our descent from manners.

Where are the people whose example we can admire and ape? Nobility is in short supply in 21st century Britain. Those who prosper feel little need to behave in an elegant, stately way. Paralysed by ill-guided notions of egalitarianism, we have lost the aspiration to inspire our fellow subjects by setting a good example.

We have developed a national aversion to excellence and it has thrown us into a spiral of "grottification" and "oikery", bad language, fecklessness, behavioural malaise. This is a spiral in which a deputy prime minister can cavort with Tracey from the office – cheating on his long-suffering wife – and sneer at faint hearts old-fashioned enough to find his behaviour coarse. It is a spiral in which bevvied-up young women in high heels clack-clack-clack into the winter streets at night because they have been reared to respect high-profile ladettes. Militant feminism becomes less liberating for a young woman when she has overdone it on pints of lager and is shivering in a city centre on Friday night in a skimpy dress.

This is a spiral in which state-subsidised theatre companies promote violent plays littered with the f-word, a spiral in which the very idea of impressive, high-minded elitism – that is, the best, be it in art or politics or in any other area of human endeavour – has been disowned by a ruling class allergic to privilege while happily hooked on perks.

We are told, without so much as a hat-tip to the Orwellian satire, that all men are equal. You do not have to be a raging Thatcherite (I happen not to be) to argue that, in fact, all men and women are not equal. All men and women are different and thank goodness for that. Without it we would be clones and would probably have succumbed to some simple genetic disease.

Disparities in ability make good manners all the more desirable. They are an acknowledgment, by the lucky, of their good fortune and they are a compensation, no matter how slight, for those who have been less favoured by fate. This is why militant egalitarians are suspicious of good manners. They consider such charm a plot, an affront, a leftover of less democratic times, a relic of feudalism. We are told that judgmentalism is wrong and that all "lifestyles" are valid. Is it therefore any surprise that the rich have come to the selfish decision that they need do nothing for the society in which they live?

When all people are equal, why should beady-eyed plutocrats show any obligation to the poor and needy? How does that make us more democratic or fair? Quite the opposite, surely. In a country which is forever being told that all people are equal, no one needs to try to live to a code of manners and distinction. And thus it has come to pass. Parliament bubbled and boiled like a sub-tropical swamp, its disputatious members mired in expenses scandals. Need I remind you of the second-home allowance fiddles, the literally incredible mileage claims, the hiring of lovers and relations at the taxpayers' expense? We used to consider corruption Third World. Suddenly it was here, in London SW1, supposed fount of parliamentary civilisation. Yikes. This happened in little more than a generation. It does not take long for brambles to climb up and colonise the temple. If we neglect manners, the citadel soon becomes as covered in thorns as was Sleeping Beauty's castle.

British politics, far from being the noble art of public service, suddenly looked more like a grand prix of larceny and gobby knavishness. Dishonesty became pervasive, like the smell of rotting mouse. Spin doctors went forth and multiplied, sidling along the corridors of the Palace of Westminster, talking out of the sides of their mouths into mobile telephones as they planted rumours and stoked discontent. The Government information machine was bent out of shape. Simultaneously, many of Parliament's powers were diluted or dispensed, be it to new-fangled agencies of government or to the European Union. Responsibility (a prerequisite for a system of manners) withered. Shame, in the post-modern age, was reserved not for bad manners but for failure to observe political correctness. It was perfectly in order to cheat on your spouse and swear and swagger but Heaven help you if you called an Inuit an Eskimo or a Sioux a Red Indian.

The House of Commons from 1997 to 2010 reached a historic low. It may be no coincidence that, as the nation's legislature slipped into moral torpor, public behaviour deteriorated. I do not mean eating in the streets and men failing to open doors for women. It has been more violent than that. I mean the sort of medium-level menace now found on late-night trains, road rage, juveniles' scurviness to the old, and the effing and blinding aimed at police officers – a practice which has been condoned as everyday by a member of the judiciary, Mr Justice Bean.

The contrarian could argue that Parliament's grimy ways merely show how in tune our politicians are with their electors, how representative they are of the nation they claim to govern. Is it not equally likely that the country took one look at what was going on at the bad old House of Commons and reckoned: "Well, if they're going to behave badly, why shouldn't I?" As a parliamentary sketchwriter, I must confess that I rather rely on MPs to shout and scream at the weekly Prime Minister's Question Time. A chamber of armpit-scratching chimps makes fun copy and they have certainly kept me in spuds these recent years. But I am not sure their misconduct does much for public order. Exactly how is their heckling and partisanship different from that of football hooligans? There is a decent philosophy thesis to be had in that question.

Parliament's failings have been cheerfully reported by the press but the fourth estate, alas, is little better. From phone hacking to paparazzi stalkers, by way of wild hyperbole and bias, the media emit a stink as sulphurous as bad duck-eggs. Perhaps it was ever thus – journalism is hardly an occupation for monks – but the clash with Parliament has led to febrile demands for revenge and the press now faces calls for its censure. As the Roman poet Juvenal asked: "*Quis custodiet ipsos custodes?*" (who will guard the guards?). Who will regulate the press? Once we might have been able to rely on the public to do that, but what if today's public has so little idea of propriety that it has lost the ability to discriminate? In a Fleet Street where all readers are equal, distinctions between tabloid and broadsheet have diminished. Some days, the only real difference between a "quality" and a "popular" paper is the calibre of the crossword. News values are almost identical. The free market, I'm afraid, has not done much to defend genteel manners.

Shielding our little ones' eyes, let us cast elsewhere for beacons of decency. The civil service? Once the realm of dry bods of actuarial and procedural bent, it is today unrecognisable as an acme of inky administration. It is now not so much a Rolls-Royce as a smoking Ford Mondeo. Whitehall cock-ups abound. Inefficiency snowballs with a well-fed sense of departmental inertia because, well, no one expects any better. To demand higher standards is to be "snobbish", at which word the *gauleiters* of the commentariat hurl high their hands in horror. How out of date those episodes of *Yes, Minister* seem with their exquisite phrasing and their niceness of nuance. Sir Humphrey, who until the Eighties was regarded as a stickler for form and intellectual exactitude, has become a greyshoed middler, a trundler in hock to jargon. Precision of thought and rigorous independence have been dropped – too elitist, you see.

The law? Surely its practitioners are beyond reproach. Actually, perhaps not. One glance at the world of personal injury solicitors – the dreaded ambulance chasers – is enough to challenge the strongest stomach. Judges have had their powers of discretion reduced in the name of egalitarian fairness. Magistrates are sent on courses to drum the middle-class values out of them. The ancient bulwark of the Law Lords went. They were zapped and replaced by an allegedly more "accountable" Supreme Court which is nothing of the sort and never comes anywhere near the established forum of Parliament. Where once we had the law embodied physically by a full-bottom wigged Lord Chancellor, the grandee's grandee but a creature of the electorate, now we have an obscure cadre of silks. At the Supreme Court they wear gowns which look vaguely European and utilitarian, like upmarket lavatory attendants. More egalitarian, less enlightening, less open, less equal, in the sense of being close to the great unwashed British populace.

Nor is there much reassurance to be found among the accountants, certainly not the big City firms which charge such rapacious fees, often under the bluffing guise of management consultancy. Or should we look to banking for our heroes? Puh-lease. Captain Mainwaring, manager of the town bank in *Dad's Army*'s Walmington-on-Sea, was a stalwart of civic values, a volunteer, a pillar of admittedly slightly pompous propriety. He has been replaced by something less class-conscious but more opaque. This is not progress.

How about the Church? Anglicanism retains a few pockets of top-end grandeur – its cathedrals are enjoying an under-acknowledged boon, and if for nothing else we must worship the outgoing Archbishop of Canterbury, Dr Rowan Williams, for that magnificent Old Testament beard. If you potted that thing, it could cover a conservatory as quickly as a clematis. But the Church of England is, on the whole, a dismayingly wet tent these days. Even in 1977, when the Stranglers were at their work, wearers of episcopal purple tended to be distinguished men of prayer. Today many of them are social workers first, princes of the Church second. "Accessible" happy-clappy hymns have replaced the muscular snorters of Empire days. The awe-inducing language of the *Book of Common Prayer* has been disowned in many dioceses, replaced by words and phrases which are no more elevated than the plastic menu at a Wimpy burger bar. Where is the majesty? Where is the dignity of the old middle-stump Anglican restraint?

Art, once, was a forum for expert execution, its disciplines being the intellectual symbol of achievement and a representation of beauty, or at least of truth. No more. If art becomes secondary to schlock-horrordom, why should any talented young artist bother to study? Are yacky, yappy manners the route to riches? The egalitarians who hail Tracey Emin and her ilk do so because they weaken the legitimacy of the order of line which allowed us indisputably to rate some artists above others. What their destruction has done, apart from cheapening sensation, is rip away opportunity for unknown youngsters who might have been able to flourish as a result of their God-given ability. Egalitarian zeal and piggy-backing on rudeness has damaged the very people it should hope to help.

Can we find heroes elsewhere? In the Square Mile? The City's elders and grandees would once have placed a high premium on their reputations but old gauges of respectability in the livery companies and around the court of the Bank of England have been trashed and mocked by modernisers. And so the old City has retreated and our counting houses are now less answerable to the wider world. With the diminishing of aldermanic protocols, society has lost some of its purchase on the bonus boys. They might as well sing the chant of Millwall football supporters: "No one likes us, we don't care."

Do we cast our gaze to the portals of the Premier League, home to some of the richest young men in the land and remark on their sporting decency? I think not. They spit on the pitch. They argue with the ref. And they treat their girlfriends like disposable objects.

Do we switch on the television to find heroes? Jeremy Clarkson, perhaps, or Jonathan Ross or Frankie Boyle or Russell Brand? Ye gods. The BBC, chasing ratings, abjures politeness and tries to scandalise. In doing so it fails in its proper function, which should be to elevate society and nurture intelligence. Yet any such elevation involves calculations about intellectual superiority. Oooh, we can't be doing with that. And so they give us tat instead of art. They give us phone-ins instead of straight news. Their weather forecasters speak in babyish, provincial voices rather than in the crisp, dispassionate Queen's English of yesteryear. All this is done because they live in dread of sounding well-mannered and elitist.

Much as I sometimes enjoy Jeremy Paxman's derisive tone when he is interviewing Cabinet ministers and Opposition spokesmen, is this good for our national culture? Might there not be a link between the contempt Paxo and other top interviewers show our leaders and, say, the contempt we see shown to ticket collectors by young fare-dodgers on the trains? The complex kingdom of manners depends on notions of better and worse. You can, if you like, call that class or rank or hierarchy – as the BBC and its default egalitarians do – or you could call it self-interest. A Britain shorn of social grades is weaker. It is baffled. It cries out for leadership.

Is our Prime Minister the answer? I wish I could say yes with greater confidence. When Mr Cameron set out to rebrand the Conservative Party in 2005 he urged his male colleagues to stop wearing ties. The relaxed, open-necked look had become *de rigueur*. That swanky Tory fundraiser in Battersea previously known as the Black and White Ball became an event at which Nehru jackets almost outnumbered dinner jackets, and those DJs were worn *sans* dicky bows, even at the start of the evening. In fact the event was no less swanky. It was still stuffed with county gals and babbling Berties. The difference was that, without their bow ties, they looked less posh, less hoity toity. The camera never lies? Of course it does. It lied that night.

Tiegate was a piffling episode, you might think. But Mr Cameron's chasing of a dumbed-down image was dismaying. It suggested that he lacked the self-confidence to be what he is – the son of privilege. We inhabit a strange world in which it is somehow acceptable to run from grandeur, abdicate leadership. The tieless Cameroons were trying to appear everyone's best mates. That might work in Opposition but it becomes a great deal less feasible when those best mates are in power. The requirement now that they have indeed won office is for sobriety, semi-judicial gravity. Oh no! Bring back the old-fashioned ties!

Bring them back, by all means. It would not be too difficult. There are other ways we could easily retrieve, or at least nurture, some of our heroes. All is not yet lost.

Let us demand that sporting stars behave as such – that is, by being sporting. The drug-taking and the cheating found in so many professional sports, from tennis to once honourable rugby union, must stop. We have it in our power to enforce this. Society will change if society demands better.

Football receives a lot of state support. Very well. Let that support be given on the basis that the Football Association puts a stop to the professional fouls and the loutish behaviour. Football influences the way children behave. It has a social responsibility. If strikers happen to score a goal they should limit themselves to a congratulatory handshake, as Bobby Charlton once did, rather than sprinting to the corner flag, clenched fist aloft, snarling foul words of self-acclaim. If the game is unwilling to change, let some of those players be invited to a parliamentary select committee to answer questions from MPs. That chastening technique has been spectacularly effective with errant newspaper executives. Let it be tried now on the fat cats of soccer.

Let us demand an end to crudeness in programmes spewed out by state-licensed broadcasters. Let us shame newspapers that snoop on grieving families and chase actresses down alleys for a snatched photograph. Let us also stick it to the production companies which organise the emotional show trials of daytime trash TV. Let us stiffen the arm of the British Board of Film Classification. But let us not bring in privacy laws which would excuse the media from making life pretty hot for fraudulent, greedy bankers.

Let us demand some fire and brimstone from our prelates and assure them that morality can be a liberating force, particularly for those at the bottom of the social scale. Let us deplore the wider availability of casino gambling, which impoverishes the already poor and enriches only the already rich. And let us question some of the sarcasm in British humour. By all means let us continue to mock, but let us reserve our mockery for those who deserve it rather than Rotary Club members and morris dancers and bell ringers and spinsters and the Variety Sunshine Coaches passengers picked on by "funnymen".

We can make a start. We can hail politeness as liberal, Left-wing and Right, as an essential lubricant to both personal happiness and civic harmony. But we will not achieve these things without heroes.

Quentin Letts is a journalist and theatre critic who frequently lets rip at the state of modern society in columns in the Daily Mail. He lives with his wife and three children in Herefordshire, where he likes to sing hymns and watch cricket.

CHAPTER EIGHT

DRESSING DOWN FOR DINNER
Liz Jones, on what to wear when

Conjure the scene. The hallowed library of the Cambridge Union Society on a wintry night. The invitation clearly states "black tie". The president of the debating club, an apple-cheeked young woman with Mary Hopkin hair, is in a long dress. The young men are in dark suits. Some have bow ties. I remember there is nothing more appealing than extreme youth buttressed against formal attire. I, as a guest speaker and someone educated in a polytechnic astride the Elephant and Castle, have given great thought to my outfit and am wearing a black tailcoat by Sarah Burton for Alexander McQueen, a black and gold lace couture skirt by London designer Suzannah, with black Prada shoes and handbag. My handbag, given it is now past 6pm, is suitably small, my heels fashionably high. I am nervous, and always cover my fears by making sure I am impeccably turned out. If I were a racehorse, I'd have a chequerboard pattern on my rump. I feel privileged to be here.

But isn't an atmosphere ruined by the arrival, as it is plonked on a table, of a dirty old, great big rucksack? The bag, if you can call it that, belongs to Rachel

Johnson, editor-in-chief of *The Lady*. Shouldn't she, of all people, know better? Worse is to follow. Fellow panellist Katie Price arrives. She is wearing sparkly black treggings that reveal every contour of those magnificent legs and buttocks. A black sweater, over which is pulled a sort of grey jerkin. Very high boots. And very long, blonde extensions.

Now, while I love a drawstring waist as much as the next woman, the lack of thought that now goes into getting dressed for any occasion, let alone dinner, manages to scupper even the most carefully planned of occasions. At my wedding, a country one at Babington House but a formal occasion nonetheless, one of my brothers turned up in jeans and cowboy boots. "I don't like weddings," he moaned. "But this is the one day that is supposed to be about me!" I wailed. At the funeral of a relative in Scotland, the deceased's widower wore… a cream blouson and deck shoes! And stubble! Men in particular really have no excuse for dressing inappropriately, given the price of a black single-breasted suit in Marks & Spencer.

Fashion is always seen as something frivolous and irrelevant. But to be well groomed and smart involves discipline. Even when my dad was 80, and suffering from cancer, he managed every day to wear crisp slacks, an ironed shirt (never short-sleeved) and polished brogues. He learned this rigour in the British Army, and in the Sixties regarded the long hair and pungent afghans of my three older brothers as indicative of a society that was going to the dogs.

Footage of the English riots during the summer of 2011 revealed that is exactly what happened to this once great nation. The rioters wore grey sweats with hoodies, sneakers and – a new one on me – pyjama bottoms, surely the ultimate symbol of indolence, of opting out. Gone was any sense of bling, which came into fashion in the black US ghettos in the late Seventies, an ironic statement on its wearer's lack of credit worthiness. Instead they wore the great big logos of Ivy League universities, courtesy of Abercrombie & Fitch, surely a sartorial slap in the face given its wearer will never row, or wield a baseball bat other than to use it on someone else's head. Not one of these rioters, upon getting dressed, had had to wield an iron, or even a shoe brush. These clothes engender a posture, too: a bouncy walk, a collapsed middle, which in turn affects the brain. While the women's corset was heinous, and replaced by the flapper dresses of the Twenties, it was soon resurrected in many ways over the next few years: women's dresses had bones, darts, seams and lining. There was no "give" in fabric, not until the invention of Lycra in the Sixties. But now it has gone too far, with too much leeway, in every sense of the word. Women are expected to have the bodies of Olympic athletes in order to wear that Calvin Klein sheer nude slip, with no help in the control department at all. While men, having never fastened a button, have no control, no staying power, no rigour.

Today, absolutely anything goes, all over the world. I remember I once went on holiday to Las Vegas. The image in my mind was one of Frank Sinatra and Sammy Davis, Jr: narrow ties; fedoras at a jaunty angle; dark single-breasted Brioni suits. What did I find instead? Tracksuits in pastels; shorts on grown men whose only culture was back fat. And I had thought American men to be like Niles Crane in *Frasier*, or *The Thin Man*, played so gloriously by William Powell in the 1934 film. Or Cary Grant, who demonstrated how to execute casual wear so brilliantly in *To Catch a Thief*.

A morning spent recently at the ITV headquarters on the South Bank in London revealed young women in denim shorts over coloured tights. Armpits, both male and female. Flip flops. Floral tea dresses over jeans. Vests. String vests. And sequins which, according to "style queen" Rachel Zoe – the woman who gave us the ideal of big head, tiny body covered in kaftan over white jeans, super-sized sunnies, and a tote the size of a hippo – are "OK for day". The overriding impression was not of young professionals off to work, but of teenagers on a binge-drinking package holiday.

Does it really matter, this propensity for wearing something that is easiest for you, but often disrespectful of others? People will nearly always cite expense and lack of time as the reason they don't dress smartly. But I have spent time in a slum in Dhaka where, every morning, women and children emerge pressed and clean, to know that poverty or fatigue, or lack of time, are never an excuse. These garment factory workers and their children know that without self-respect, they have nothing. If you do not bother to iron your shirt or dress, if you're showing me your toe cleavage or, worse, the fact you still (still?) wear a red thong, then you are disrespecting me, the unfortunate who has to sit next to you in the office or on the bus.

But of course we now have a new assault on our sensibilities: the hyper-groomed. Hyper-grooming has infected young women the length and breadth of Britain, and involves long, highlighted extensions, nails blighted with little sequins and kittens, a skin the colour of my mother's sideboard (the texture is similar, too), moist lips, pancaked face, no hair on the body to speak of so it refracts lights like a disco ball, and eyelashes so heavy they give the wearer a sleepy expression.

They should be tired, given the amount of time and expense this hyper-grooming requires. These girls all wear Carvela wedges and tiny strips of Lycra across private parts that have been rendered prepubescent with hot wax, and vajazzled with rhinestones, a sort of landing strip for the equally tanned, over-aerobicised young males who are too ignorant to know the location of anything, let alone a G-Spot (which these girls think stands for Gucci).

This new look sprung out of a weird cocktail of new technology (I mean the gel pedicure, not the iPhone 5), disenfranchisement due to the recession and a new breed of role models – Rihanna, Cheryl Cole, Tulisa, hell, even Adele, the only curvy poster girl for our time – who believe themselves to be post-feminist, abandoning the more natural look of a Carole King, say, to become dolls. But to me they are mere victims, doppelgangers, with no taste or style of their own. The dress code for any provincial nightclub or bar these days is a dress the size of a handkerchief, no coat – these young women do not own coats – and no hanky, either, matching underwear from La Perla or Myla for "inner poise", and bare legs that can no longer indicate they are cold by bristling their hairs.

But it is not just the hyper-groomed who have been brainwashed. It is most young women. It all began back in 1998, when the first episode of *Sex and the City* was aired. From that moment, secretaries, nurses and PRs on £25,000 a year believed they too were entitled to a Fendi Baguette worth £500, or a pair of Manolo heels for £700. Oh, how fast we learned. We became Fashion Literate. Seduced by L'Oréal ads, we believed we were "worth it", which meant we now had the right not only to shop but to pamper! The new pastime for women is to spend vast amounts of money "treating" themselves to be mauled by "therapists".

Sex and the City, which did indeed feature a vast, ever changing, eclectic, wonderful wardrobe upon the narrow back of actress Sarah Jessica Parker, a US size two, was supposed to be about friendship, liberation and selfishness: three things women are often sadly lacking. Refreshingly, it was not about men, babies and housework. I only ever spied SJP once in a pair of yellow Marigolds. She never cooked, either, which wins top marks in my book now that so many women feel obliged to schedule "bake from scratch and decorate cupcakes" into their super-busy days. But unfortunately the marketeers got hold of Carrie Bradshaw's signature branding and style, spawning a slew of adverts featuring giggling gaggles of girlfriends wearing polka dots and prom dresses (my God, how I hate retro fashion, the most disempowering of all).

In the face of all this ubiquitous shopping, the luxury labels, which in 2000 were quite happy to plaster their logo upon anything, suddenly, I would say by 2005, became a little frightened. Allow too many Laurens from Basildon to wear your designer biker jacket, and the cool people, the skinny people, the really rich people, will go elsewhere. And so the luxury labels came up with a ruse. The first was to capitalise on the mania for bags and shoooooooes! Lovely shoooooesssss! These became ever bigger, ever more embellished. Not so much shoes, as

British *Vogue*'s Alexandra Shulman announced after yet
another season when models fell on the runway like so
many thoroughbreds at Becher's Brook, but "works of
art". A red-soled pair of cream Mary Janes at Christian
Louboutin can cost up to £900. A pair of ultra-high
black patent platforms with an eight-inch dagger of a
heel by Louboutin, can cost several thousands. And so we
have the New New Luxury, as perfectly summed up by a
Victoria Beckham bag made from alligator skin, costing
£19,000. Yes.

A new dress code for the Royal Enclosure at Royal
Ascot was announced for 2012. No more strapless dresses. And no more dreadful fascinators. I think we need a
new code, too, for every aspect of life. Not one as dicta-
torial as Queen Elizabeth I's, which stated that everyone
over the age of seven must wear a hat on Sundays and
holidays, but pretty strict, nonetheless.

Let's get men out of the way first. No trainers, unless
you are actually out jogging, and even then I'd rather
you went to a proper running track rather than alarming me on the pavement (I don't like joggers). Next, no
suit should ever be worn two days in a row. At night,
it should be sponged clean, and left to hang and air. If
it becomes shiny, you need to pop it in a recycling bin
without a backwards glance. Shoes should be leather, and
polished, and again never worn two days in a row. Wear
a tie and always the most expensive plain shirt you can

afford, never one that is blue on the body, white at the neck. You can wear inky Levi's at the weekend, and a V-necked (never round, far too womany) sweater. Skinny jeans will murder your sperm. Do not cover your head with a hoodie because I want to check that you have shaved. Do not wear a baseball cap, even if you are Leonardo DiCaprio, because when you lean towards me I risk being jabbed in the eye.

Now. Travel. Anywhere. Do not view the aeroplane or indeed the Tube or the bus as a place for that maggot-shaped fleece. Do not sit next to me if you are wearing synthetics on your feet, or your armpit is at liberty: you will soon hum. Do not turn round, ever, if you have a rucksack, because you will fell me like a skittle. Do not allow your children to wheel their own tiny, cute embellished pink suitcases that threaten to trip me up and bruise my shins.

That old rule that you should dress for the job you want, not the one you have, holds fast. Receptionists in Manhattan are far better turned out than most of the women in this country who are on boards of FTSE 100 companies. The newest style dictator in the UK, Mary Portas, bemoaned not long ago the fact women in government are "badly dressed". She is right. It is snobby to say you shop only in Marks, and have no time. You represent me around the world, so please set an example to all those women who get out of bed every morning and struggle into a neat black dress and tailored jacket.

I was once turned away from a restaurant at the Hotel Villa San Michele near Florence because I was wearing jeans. "Listen, these are Paper Denim & Cloth and cost £700," I told the uncomprehending waiter. Price is no excuse for being inappropriate. If you have been invited to dinner, either in someone's home (please take a gift) or in a restaurant, do not wear jeans. Actually, I always think a pretty dress or skirt so much more fitting for a woman in the evening. I hate all this talk of going from office to party, just by adding a pair of chandelier earrings (do not wear these, as they distort your lobes). Just get changed! For dinner. You will enjoy it so much more.

Finally, now that we don't, *Downton Abbey* fashion, change for dinner anymore, there are still two occasions that are formal. The first is a wedding. As a guest, it is your duty to purchase something new and smart and please, do not carry the misshapen bag you use every day for work. You need a small, rigid clutch (it will improve your posture, too). I believe shoes and bags should match, and there must be a zing of colour somewhere, if only on your mouth. A kitten heel will prevent you from making a scene, particularly if there are cobbles. Wear a hat, not something that looks like a nasty insect, and no false eyelashes, please. They will detract from the bride. Green is unlucky. Black is fine for everyone apart from the bride.

A funeral requires that everyone wear black, although if you are a man you must not wear a black shirt because then you will look, in my dad's words, like a spiv. Cover up those breasts and arms: a Spanish shawl in silver provides lovely contrast and cover. I went to my sister-in-law's funeral recently, held in Edinburgh. I wore a black Alaia wool dress under a duchesse silk opera coat with bracelet sleeves by Suzannah. I carried a black Bottega Veneta woven clutch, and wore Prada heels, patent ones for a touch of joy. My sister-in-law loved fashion, and it was my job to look my best for my two young nieces.

Above all, plan what you will wear the next day, and get the outfit out ready. Try to make every event an occasion. I sometimes walk my dogs in jodhpurs, a vivid parachute silk Katharine Hamnett shirt I've owned since 1983 that is like a jaunty flag, a navy Balmain military coat with gold buttons, a snood knitted by my mum, and pre-loved Marni biker boots. My step has more spring, my dogs more barks. And life seems different, somehow better.

Liz Jones is a journalist and the former editor of Marie Claire. She has made a name for herself writing very personal columns for newspapers and magazines and has been called the Countess of Confessional Journalism. She lives in Somerset with her pets.

CHAPTER NINE

PASS THE PORT
Giles Coren, on table manners

For quite a long part of my childhood our family home had three live-in servants: a nanny, a cook and a house-keeper. The last two were Italian sisters who had answered an advertisement in *The Lady* for a cook/housekeeper and were happy to share a salary and an apartment in our big Thirties house tucked into the armpit of Finchley Road and the A41, in suburban North London. They had been in service in "great houses" for 50 years, and as opportunities for domestic staff gradually disappeared after the War they were happy to meld into a single employee rather than retire or be separated.

But still, three servants. Pretty bloody *Downton Abbey* for London in the Seventies, especially for a middle-class professional couple: a humorous writer and an anaesthetist.

Add to that a gardener, Kerridge (he insisted on only his surname being used – I have no idea what his first name was), and a daily cleaner, and then Les, the milkman who always stopped in for a cup of tea and a slice of cake, and assorted bi-weekly deliveries from the butcher, grocer and greengrocer, always to the back door, the brown-coated drivers generally pausing for a flirt and a natter in the kitchen, and there was an undeniably Edwardian thing going on, considering how late it was in the century.

Lunch at weekends and dinner every evening were taken in the dining room. My father sat at the head of the table and, I kid you not, rang a little bell for courses to be brought and dishes taken away. My father, a Jewish boy, son of a Southgate plumber, married to the daughter of Slovakian Holocaust refugees, enjoying a lifestyle – thanks to a smart wit, grammar school and a raft of scholarships – that was a gentle (and surely deliberate) pastiche of pre-War English gentility.

For the children this meant rules. Dreamed up by the parents and enforced by the nanny. It was as much like the home of the Banks family at 17 Cherry Tree Lane in *Mary Poppins* as you can get without a dancing chimney sweep and penguin waiters.

There was no "answering back" and no "contradicting". Teeth were brushed three times a day and after each brushing an inspection was carried out – my sister and I lined up like two little von Trapps – by the overseeing adult. Bath time was at 6.30pm and if you weren't clean, dry and ready for bed by the time the theme music started for *The Six Million Dollar Man* at seven, then you weren't allowed to watch it at all (a bizarre penalty, since the opening credits were the best bit).

We were to respect our father "because I'm your

father" and to do things "because I say so". We were even told (possibly not entirely seriously – though it's too long ago now to be sure) that we should be "seen and not heard".

Deviation from accepted rules of behaviour was punished by whacks. Not brutality or abuse. But whacks. Quite hard whacks.

But of all rules, none were so formally codified as the rules of table manners. Standard Victorian etiquette was to be observed at all times, whether it was formal meals at the long, mahogany dining table in the main dining room, with the Tenniel drawings and the Regency sideboard and the collection of early English delftware, or kitchen suppers (or lunches or breakfasts) in the cork and Formica kitchen next door:

1. No eating with your mouth open.
2. No talking with your mouth full. These two were very easily confused in a young mind to create a sort of etiquette spoonerism: "Don't talk with your mouth open or eat with your mouth full." For years, until really quite recently, I had to mutter the respective legislation under my breath to be sure I had it the right way round.
3. No elbows on the table. This one having the dread whiff of Divine Command about it. Although not practising Jews, we did go to Passover every year at my maternal grandparents' house in Stanmore,

where the prayer book (*Haggadah*) makes a big deal about how on this night, as opposed to all other nights, we may "lean". I never got to the bottom of why we were allowed to lean on Passover, but I did absorb the fact that on the other 364 nights of the year we were not allowed to lean our elbows on the table BECAUSE GOD SAYS SO. (We were not, in actuality, allowed to lean our elbows on the table on Passover either – because table manners, for nice children, in posh houses, are more important than God).

4. Hands nicely in your lap between mouthfuls. A big one with my mother, this one. I suppose it is meant to be more dainty, but it felt very weird to be forced to chew without touching ones cutlery. Like riding a bicycle without touching the handlebars. You never see anybody doing it now. It's quite ridiculous.

5. Cut the meat, don't tear it. This was a battle that went on for years.

6. Drink soup from the side of the spoon, not the front. Or possibly the other way round. Whichever is the more difficult.

7. No drinks with soup. This was one of my dad's. Apparently soups are wet so you don't need another liquid. We drank orange squash as a rule, and it sat there in the jug, waiting for us to finish our soup.

8. Chew properly before you swallow. There was even a period when my parents genuinely proposed that we chew 30 times and count each one (in our heads obviously, to avoid breaking rules 1 and 2) before swallowing. They said this was what certain people recommended for better digestion. Thirty years later I finally re-encountered this bonkers notion when filming *Edwardian Supersize Me*, in which Sue Perkins and I briefly pursued the "chew-chew" diet invented by Horace Fletcher, and I received confirmation that my family's aspirations had been every bit as strictly Edwardian as I had imagined.

9. Don't reach, ask. Or better still, wait to be offered. My mother said that in nice houses nobody ever asks for anything, such as salt or pepper or more squash, you just sit there and wait till it's offered. "But what if nobody offers?" I would ask. "Then they are very rude," she would reply. "Maybe so," I would reply (stepping perilously close to the "answering back" line), "but you might be desperate for a drink." In which case, apparently, you were to say to the person next to you, "May I pass you anything?" to which they would reply "No thank you. May I pass YOU anything?" And then you would ask if it wasn't too much trouble to beg a little water. This utterly ridiculous system

only works if everybody knows about it, of course. Just this Christmas, at a table of 12, I heard my mother ask: "May I pass anybody anything?" And everybody just carried on eating, elbows on table, mouths open, one or two of them muttering, "No thanks, I'm fine", and it was probably a minute before I realised what she meant, heard a voice from 30 years ago whispering to me, and said, "No thank you, Mummy, may I pass you something?" It turned out she wanted the sprouts.

10. Finish what is in front of you or you're having it for breakfast. Massive one this. Citing either starving babies in Africa, or their own childhoods during rationing, my parents made it the highest moral issue of all, that not a morsel be left on the plate. In those years of home dining, "gristle" was my greatest enemy. Many evenings were spent staring at a thick belt of pork fat (as I said, we were not *that* Jewish) which I could not imagine swallowing, but without swallowing which I would not be allowed to go to bed. If it was still there at bath time it was taken away, and presented to me in the morning for breakfast. Honestly. It's why I eat everything in sight now. Can't leave a thing. Nor throw any food away in the kitchen, gobbling down whatever is in the pot and scraping it clean and eating the scrapings before washing up. My wife thinks it is an ill-

ness, and I talk endlessly to my psychoanalyst about it (yes, of course I have an analyst – you thought I came through all this unscathed?). My wife is most exasperated by the fact that she cannot cook large meals with a view to serving leftovers later in the week, because I eat every last thing before she can put it away in the fridge, twitching and cowering as I go, and worrying that I won't be allowed to go to bed unless I do.

11. Don't get up from the table without asking. And don't even bother asking unless you have complied with rule 10.

12. No eating between meals. Because it will "spoil your appetite". A ridiculous notion for so many reasons: appetite exists to be sated; to arrive at a major meal starving hungry will spoil your enjoyment of it; it is healthier to eat little and often. (Here I am, answering back with glee, now that my father is dead.)

13. No mixing of cereals. Truly. No two cereals to be put in the same bowl together. Like some bizarre little rule of *kosher* right at the very end of God's interminable list of prohibitions. Throughout my childhood I dreamed of mixing Coco Pops and Alpen, but it was more strictly forbidden than murder. I have no idea why. Perhaps because food was not supposed to be fun. I wondered if there

were some sort of terrible chemical reason – perhaps there would be a nuclear explosion if Frosties, say, came into contact with Ricicles.

And the list goes on and on. So many rules, so many variations of rules. And it was the only guidance we got. Our parents offered no other ethical instruction. No other guidelines for the living of life. All that mattered was our table manners. They were a pure and applicable distillation of all the general morality that man had devised, and from them all decency and personal rectitude flowed, at home and abroad.

As I grew older, they had no problem with me smoking, drinking, drinking and driving, taking drugs (hard or soft), fighting, getting done for shoplifting, affray, possession, resisting arrest, working endless years as a barman and shop assistant, screwing around and refusing to get a proper job, failing to start a family... all these were boyish high jinks that would iron themselves out as I grew up, and nothing to do with morality, decency or being a gentleman. But fail to say, "This is delicious chicken, mother, you must tell me the recipe," or reach for the wine bottle at lunch without getting up to pour everybody else first and... pow! A clip round the ear, oldskool, right through into my twenties. Because western civilisation depended on table manners, and on nothing else at all.

It wasn't until I was about 15 that I realised my father's own table manners were appalling. He chewed and slurped and scarfed his food like a waste disposal unit breaking up a chicken, and he talked all the while, forking the food into his still-talking mouth like an engine driver stoking the boiler. All this with his head leaning lazily on his elbow-propped fist, pointing at the things he wanted passed to him with the fork hand – relishing, clearly, his own appetite and trencherman's enthusiasm for the table, flecks of food spinning from his lips to the tablecloth as he spoke.

But one wasn't allowed to say anything, because above even table manners on the list of injunctions, up where even God did not dare raise a question, was the rule about respecting your father. It was a tightly ordered domestic structure of the sort that Jane Austen's favourite moralist, Edmund Burke, considered essential to the maintenance of English society and to the resistance of Jacobinism. And she knew a bit about manners, did Miss Austen.

When I eventually did settle down to a job, cracked on to writing and broadcasting like any other man finally accepting a dull position in the family firm, it is probably not surprising that I quite quickly turned to writing about eating habits.

I became a restaurant critic first of all for *Tatler* – the very almanac of table manners and of etiquette generally. And then for *The Independent* and then, finally, for

The Times, apogee of all that is well mannered, correct, decent, traditional and at the same time ever so slightly critical and proscriptive. There is no question that whatever else my parents' obsession with table manners did, whatever weird eating disorders it bequeathed to my sister and me, it got me a job.

And so now every week I tell people how to eat. Not in the bourgeois sense of how to comport themselves at table so as to pass for "better" than they are (although I am still upset by the sight of grown men and women holding their knife all dainty like a pen, as far back on the stem as possible, dangling the cutlery ineffectively over the plate as if the further from the food one keeps one's hand the more polite one is) but in the sense of where to do it and what to eat there and what to drink with it.

In the very beginning of restaurants, in the early 19th century, they were designed to mimic meals in grand houses. Then, after the Second World War, people serving meals at home tried more and more to imitate the way it was done in restaurants, so that my parents' generation stuck rigidly to three plated courses served at table, often through an actual hatch. Now, in the past ten years, restaurants have come full circle to imitate the way we eat at home when we are at our most relaxed: one course, served centrally on sharing plates, everyone dig in, lots of wine, lots of chat, lots of laughs, lots of

leaning, talking, shouting, maybe stick the telly on. No
rules at all. None. Because meal times are where we have
fun now, above all. The Lord of Misrule is, after all these
years, back at the head of the table as he was in the very
beginning when we gathered round the woolly mammoth
carcass and it was every man for himself.

But there are still rules for good behaviour in restaurants, if not for how and when and how many times you
must chew.

1. Be polite and kind to the staff. That's fundamen-
    tal. However casually you treat each other at the
    table, these soppy little Eastern Europeans tak-
    ing your order are sad, lonely, underpaid and a
    long way from home. Look them in the eye when
    you talk to them, don't mutter while staring at
    the menu and expect them to overhear (women,
    especially, I implore you to tell the waiter what
    you want and not, as so many of you seem to,
    the nearest man at your table), and say "please"
    and "thank you". These niceties do not matter
    anymore among friends. But these people are not
    your friends. They are as close as you will get to
    being waited on by servants, and some noblesse
    oblige is required. Apart from anything else,
    "please" and "thank you" are probably the only
    English they know.
2. Tip. This follows from rule 1 quite naturally, and

is to be done regardless of whether "service" is included on the bill. You are the big man or woman with the job and the car and the ready cash to spaff on overpriced food and criminally marked-up wine. You can afford it. Give the guy a tenner, or a twenty. Not because it is a percentage of anything (the silent Bulgarian student in Pizza Express is no less deserving of your largesse than the liveried flunky at The Connaught) or because he deserves it or other people are doing it (or not doing it), but because it is polite.

3. Summon the waiter with a smile and a raised hand. Not a wave, and certainly not a finger snap and above all NOT A CLAP! With the arrival of the Russians in London, descending *en masse* on (mostly) our pan-Asian clip-joints and big hotels, the finger-snap summons has rudely entered our green and pleasant land. They come here with their slipstream of prostitutes, flunkies and drug dealers, plonk themselves down and begin snapping their fingers for service like Fifties hipsters swinging along to Cliff Richard. And as for the clappers, immediate repatriation is too good for them. It is totally unacceptable to clap for service unless you are Bernard Bresslaw in *Carry On Up the Khyber*.

4. Gentlemen, sit facing the wall. Allow the lady the view of the restaurant, while you stare at the

wallpaper/mural/funky exposed brick. Women in polite society are not even aware that restaurants have walls. Most men do follow this rule but in a row of tables along the wall in any restaurant there is usually some fat, bald, impotent little man wearing a suit but no tie and sitting on the wrong side, flanked by ladies. He is rude and stupid and pointless. And he is probably thumbing his Black-Berry, which brings us to:

5. No phones, tablets, buzzers, telegraphing equip-ment or semaphore flags. You are here with a guest to eat and talk. Not to endlessly reach for your little black inadequacy badge to kowtow to your boss/wife/Venusian overlord or to check your shares, surf porn or tweet your miserable 13 followers about what you're having for dinner, which brings us to:

6. No photographing your plate. This is the scourge of the modern restaurant experience. People click-click-clicking away with their phone, little flashes going off all over the place. It used to be the Japanese, now it is bloggers. They take photos be-cause they are too bone stupid to remember what they ate and then go away and describe it later in prose. That is why they have to blog: because nobody will pay them for their words, and nobody gives a flying shit what they think.

7. If you can't make a table you have booked, cancel it. Then they can give it to someone else. You can't go complaining about table-turning, and having to provide credit card details, and never being able to get a table at a good time on a good night in a trendy place if you then go and screw it up for everybody else by booking tables and failing to show up. And besides, it's only polite.

8. Do not eat outdoors, ever. My physics teacher at school, Mr Hepburn-Scott, was a fiend for this (do not think that the manners coaching ended when I was sent off, very Edwardianly, to boarding school) and would physically assault pupils he found eating crisps between house, say, and the science block. And I stickle for this still. One eats at home and in restaurants. Nowhere else. Not an apple at the wheel of your car, not a kebab on the pavement, not a Big Mac at the bus stop, not a vile, stinky, fridge-cold no-carb shrimp sandwich on the Underground. We are not in that much of a hurry. None of us. We can wait. We are not predators anymore. We are not scrabbling berry gatherers and carrion stealers. We are not effing jackals.

9. No boring stories when they bring the pasta about how it isn't in the same league as a little place you know in Palermo where they serve food straight off their little plot of land in the ruins of a medi-

eval abbey and the owner's daughter serves the wine naked with flowers in her hair. It's not true. You're making it up. Italy is horrible.

10. No showing off how much you know about wine. Nobody cares. You are an arse.

So, do as you please at the table. Lean, gobble, snort, blab, fiddle, point, scratch, burp, fart, yawn, hold your knife like a pen, your fork like a gear stick, your spoon like a steering wheel and for all I care get up from the table without asking your host, your mum, your confessor or the Lord Almighty. But when you are in restaurants, please, be NICE. Don't spoil it for everyone else. Because there is a chance, just a chance, that I will be sitting at the next table.

Giles Coren is The Times' restaurant critic, contributing editor of Tatler and Esquire and a regular BBC presenter, most recently of Our Food on BBC Two and before that the Supersizers series with Sue Perkins. His book, How To Eat Out, was published in 2012. He lives in London with his wife, the food writer Esther Walker, and their daughter, Kitty.

HOW RUDE!

CHAPTER TEN

IT'S JUST NOT CRICKET
Jonathan Agnew, on good sportsmanship

Just when we thought that true sporting values had died forever, the London Olympics arrived in the nick of time to deliver a resounding lesson to our professional sportsmen. The 2012 Games were conducted in the manner that sport always should be – with competitors jubilant in victory, respectful and magnanimous in defeat.

Everyone who experienced the Games was left genuinely moved by the efforts of all the athletes who came to show the world what years of dedication, discipline and commitment can achieve with such humility. I am sure I am not alone in hoping that their exemplary attitude did not die with the last flickering flame of that magnificent Olympic cauldron. Sport should always be played this way, and I hope the authorities that run professional bodies and employ role models take note.

London 2012 was an uplifting and highly motivating fortnight, with that spirit carried into the Paralympics which followed. With the enormous crowds thoroughly engaged in a fair and sporting manner – there was absolutely no swearing, intimidation or yobbery – the Olympics was a true reflection of an era we thought had been lost, never to return. Back then, the concept of sports-manship was an indeterminate but vital code, once the cornerstone of all sporting encounters. In some quarters it transcended even the outcome of the match itself to the point that being called a good sport could be considered an even greater compliment than being a good player.

And yet cheating, sharp practice and bad manners have all been accepted as being an integral part of sport for as long as the first round stone was thrown at a pre-historic bat. But accepted is far removed from condoned or even tolerated; it simply means that we have always known that it goes on. This has resulted over time in the need for umpires and referees whose responsibility for ensuring that a game runs smoothly includes keeping an eye out for anything underhand and controlling the behaviour of the players.

I have no doubt that the introduction of television, and the vast sums of money it generates, has contributed significantly to the sharp decline in acceptable standards of sportsmanship. Television companies are also guilty of portraying sport as a battle in their fight to increase ratings, creating duels in the build-up and then replaying inflammatory incidents time and again. This can have the effect of glorifying unsporting conduct rather than vilifying it.

Raging football managers, their faces contorted and eyes popping with rage, regularly appear after matches to condemn the referee – there is no other walk of life in which somebody can publicly destroy another's reputation and professionalism without having to produce evidence to a court. Meanwhile, the boorish and badly behaved sportsmen do not appear to care that their rants are broadcast into living rooms all over the world – their reasoning being that everyone else does it, which makes it all right. The unedifying details of modern behaviour on Premier League football fields emerged during the 2012 court case in which the former England captain John Terry was cleared of racially abusing Anton Ferdinand of Queens Park Rangers. The shocking and abusive language that turned the air blue in Westminster Magistrates' Court appears to be commonplace on football pitches these days, and must have made any decent person who loves sport recoil with embarrassment.

The notion that you take the rough with the smooth was deeply ingrained in young cricketers even as recently as those of my generation. But the introduction of technology to cricket has torn up this code of conduct. These days, impressionable youngsters see their heroes on television brazenly and quite legitimately dispute an umpire's decision. A batsman may now over-rule the umpire and resort to computerised technology to decide his fate, and although the option to dispute the umpire's decision is available only to international cricketers playing in a televised match, anyone who doubts that this will not have a damaging influence on behaviour on our school and club playing fields is deluded. Nothing in the modern game infuriates me more.

More of that anon, because we need first to travel back in time to what is considered to be the golden age of cricket to establish that, in fact, sport was far from whiter than white then, whatever its public image might have been. For a start, cricket was based on gambling, with match fixing prevalent among the wealthy landowners who raised the teams and then placed large wagers on the outcome of the matches they organised. The appearance of WG Grace, the most famous and immediately recognisable Victorian cricketer of them all, would add thousands to the crowd wherever he travelled, so perhaps it is not surprising that The Doctor, as he was known, and his brother, Edward, became the earliest sources of sharp practice in the game. "They've come to see me bat," was one example of WG who, having been clean bowled, replaced the bails on his broken wicket and, ignoring the howls of protest, carried on with his innings. On one occasion, Edward agreed to leave the crease following a LBW decision against him only when the crowd threatened to run on to the field and carry him off. These are hardly examples of good sportsmanship, yet they occurred during the time that evokes misty-eyed and romantic nostalgia.

Football developed along similar lines to cricket. Once

a community free-for-all, in which players kicked an animal's bladder around a rough piece of land, football was introduced to the great public schools and it influenced the gentlemanly manner in which football – and its derivation that became rugby in the mid-19th century – was played. Football was enjoyed in winter by the same society folk that played cricket in summer. The word "soccer" was created by upper class students at Oxford University as an alternative to "association". (Adding –er or –ers to abbreviated words is an Oxford tradition that the cricket commentator Brian Johnston constantly employed to his great amusement. It was, after all, how Aggers was born!)

Already, as the behaviour of the Grace brothers reveals, double standards were rife within sport. This included the question of payment, for while there were already professional cricketers in existence at the time – predominately bowlers who did all the hard work – amateurs like the good doctor were not allowed to play the game for any profit. Instead, the Graces charged heavily loaded expenses and in the case of the whole team being paid £100, nine players were paid £5 each with the Grace brothers sharing the remaining £55 between them. Such scurrilous activity was an open secret and treated with a nudge and a wink, for even in those days sport needed its characters to create interest.

The worst sporting crisis there has ever been had nothing to do with money. The Bodyline cricket series of 1932/33 between Australia and England was played in such poor spirit that it very nearly severed diplomatic links between the two great rivals. England's captain, Douglas Jardine, exploited a weakness in the law that allowed his fast bowlers to hurl down a barrage of aggressive balls at the Australians' unprotected ribs, throats and heads. England's fielders were carefully placed to catch the batsmen out as they frantically fended the ball away. A number of Australians were hit and hurt, and while it was legitimate and not an example of cheating, the deliberate intimidation of batsmen in this way was against the spirit of the game.

Bodyline aside, money has become a great corrupter. It is abundantly clear that the raising of the stakes in professional sport, due largely to television broadcast rights, has had a negative impact on sportsmanship, and the overall atmosphere in which sport is played. With significantly increased rewards for success on offer, it is not surprising that the players feel the pressure to perform well, and to win. Inevitably this has encouraged unsavoury practices, such as "sledging" – which is little more than verbally abusing your opponent in a deliberate attempt to bully, distract or infuriate him – and open hostility shown towards referees. This, in turn, has filtered down to the grass roots where the worst example of what is perceived to be emulating the "real thing" is to be found on the touchlines of youth football matches up and down the country on Saturday and Sunday mornings. A monster has been created – usually, but not exclusively male – who, for five days a week is a perfectly normal individual, happily going about his everyday life. Then, when he takes his precious son for what should be the highlight of the weekend for both, this otherwise calm and decent individual morphs into a bullying, abusive and threatening maniac. No one is spared the benefit of his misplaced knowledge of the laws, or his superior coaching skills. If anyone needs to witness the grotesque downside of television's worthy attempt to make experts out of everyone, head to a park near you next weekend. I wonder how many youngsters have been driven to give up the healthy, enjoyable and innocent pastime of playing football every week through the shame and embarrassment of their father's behaviour?

Still there are isolated examples of sporting venues where an opponent's successful endeavours are genuinely appreciated. The crowds that flock to Lord's cricket ground and Wimbledon enjoy their day in the sun in very much the same way as those who happily cheered on the London Olympians, regardless of which country they were representing. However, all around the world sports crowds have become increasingly partisan. The worst I have encountered is India. There, even a four struck by an opposing batsman is met with deafening silence from the tens of thousands of people that moments earlier were cheering wildly. The fall of an Indian wicket can be an unnerving experience for the inexperienced commentator, who is used to a crescendo of noise when the bails go flying. It can really make you wonder if your eyes have deceived you.

The Barmy Army, which is the travelling band of England cricket supporters, took their partiality one step further in Australia in the winter of 2010/11 when their cruel – if amusing – song aimed at Australian bowler Mitchell Johnson reached a crescendo in Sydney. Walking out to bat, Johnson was hit by a wall of sound from thousands of England supporters chanting in unison. Visibly shaken, he was bowled first ball.

There is the finest of lines between what is acceptable crowd behaviour, supporting the home team, and what is clearly unacceptable. American Ryder Cup crowds grew increasingly hostile in the Nineties, targeting Colin Montgomerie in particular – and this in a sport in which etiquette is an essential element to its fabric. Indeed, of all the major 21st century sports, only golf has managed successfully to cling to endearing ideals. Self-policed by the players themselves, golf is striving to remain the last bastion of true sportsmanship in professional sport. Competing players are expected to join the search for the other's lost ball – even on the last fairway with a Major Championship at stake. A respectful silence is expected when your opponent is playing his shot, and tradition dictates that the winner of the Masters is helped into the famous green jacket by the man he has dethroned. That poignant symbol of defeat must be unique in sport.

And yet even in golf, standards are slipping with the great champion Tiger Woods arguably the worst offender – throwing clubs to the ground in disgust at a poor shot and even spitting on the green.

The most violent of sports still employs a code of conduct. Boxing is a highly charged duel between two supremely fit and psyched-up individuals, but both will touch gloves before the fight begins. This is a sport in which you have to earn your challenger's respect and when the bout is over, the two combatants will often collapse into each other's arms. But once again, the televising of boxing has increased the hype to breaking point. The weigh-in press conferences that Muhammad Ali used with such great effect to tease his opponents, have become surly and ignorant affairs. Ali's humour, intellect and rhetoric have been replaced by ugly threats and absurd posturing that can often spill out in the ring. Mike Tyson, one of the most destructive boxers in history, resorted to biting a piece out of Evander Holyfield's right ear and spitting it out on to the canvas. Tyson's boxing licence was suspended. Surely he should never have been allowed into a boxing ring again?

The thirst for success has led to underhand activity away from the actual field of play. Drug abuse and corruption are the two greatest threats to the integrity of sport. In both cases, as detection by the authorities becomes more successful, the criminals – for that is what they are – become wiser. Masking agents were introduced to contaminate samples, giving the impression than an athlete is clean, when he is not. Illegal bookmakers have diverted their attention in team sports from the complicated business of fixing a match, to simply influencing a small passage of a game. As we saw in the case of the Pakistan cricket team in 2010, this can be narrowed down to the bowling of a single no-ball – so innocent to the majority of sports fans, but worth a fortune in the illegal bookmaking markets in Mumbai and Dubai. These two illegal activities are sport's greatest modern enemy, and those who are found guilty must be dealt with ruthlessly, and made examples of.

How self-confessed drug cheats, such as sprinter Dwain Chambers and cyclist David Millar, were selected to compete in the 2012 Olympics is nothing short of a disgrace. What message does it send to the next generation of athletes if the Court of Arbitration for Sport in Lausanne, Switzerland, can overturn the judgment of the British Olympic Association, and potentially place one of these men on the winner's podium with that most treasured prize in sport, an Olympic gold medal, hanging round his neck. This is not a knee-jerk "throw away the key" reaction; it is only through seriously tough punishments that sport can be protected. The sanctions imposed upon the three Pakistan cricketers who were found guilty of spot betting and subsequently served prison sentences, were measured and fair. The youngest of the trio, Mohammad Amir, who was only 19 at the time, will be able to return to cricket in his mid-twenties, older and wiser for the experience. He was clearly influenced and pressurised by his captain, Salman Butt, who should be too old to play for his country ever again.

Football is the most popular sport in the United Kingdom, and yet its reputation for declining sportsmanship is easily the worst. Because of its enormous reach, this is the sport that must clean up its act for others to follow, and surely the Terry-Ferdinand court case was the nadir for the game's image. The players and their managers earn such ludicrous sums of money that handing out fines as punishments has no impact whatsoever. The only way to impose a penalty that really works is to deduct league points. That would focus the mind of a striker tempted to take a dive, or of a manager before he criticises a defenceless referee. An individual who behaves recklessly or irresponsibly would be letting down his team-mates and fans, which is very different to losing a few quid from an over-inflated bank account. And this is the procedure that all sports should impose. Penalty runs in cricket, penalty shots in golf, and so on: I would bet there would be a dramatic improvement in attitude and sportsmanship on every front.

There must be greater control over the use of technology. I concede that it might make a marginal difference to the number of correct decisions that are made in a Test match, but in a sport played by fallible human beings, that should not be the be all and end all. Technology disturbs the flow of the game, kills moments of drama stone dead and while football considers the introduction of goal-line technology, what is the sense in showing that the ball has crossed the line but that the scorer was offside in the first place? Try as hard as football might want to prevent it, technology will quickly be expanded to include off-side, fouls and penalties and the game will grind to a halt.

We were assured in the cricket world that the introduction of technology would improve sportsmanship and the standard of player behaviour. The opposite is true with batsmen still waiting to be given "out" when they have clearly edged the ball, and even disputing the decision that has been made by the computer.

But most important of all, technology undermines the umpire and the referee, which is the most alarming aspect to the declining standards of sportsmanship and decency. The respect for the game's authority, which is essential to the running of any sport, has already vanished from the football world, even without the assistance of the dreaded technology. That sad reality is there to see on television most days of the week. What chance is there of restoring proper sporting values when the role models are, quite understandably, motivated by money rather than the great pleasure and pride of pulling on their shirt?

Football holds the key; a sport in which a handshake – the most basic gesture of respect and friendship – was recently considered to be too inflammatory, and dispensed with. A sport in which players appear deliberately to attempt to have an opponent sent off and in which managers, who are not supposed to criticise referees, actually resort to accusing them of bias without recrimination.

Showing respect to an opponent or to the referee is not a sign of weakness. It is recognition of the fact that all the great sportsmen and women who grace our television screens do so alarmingly briefly. Their time in the sun is nothing compared to the longevity of the game or discipline at which they are fortunate enough to excel. It is the responsibility of every competitor to ensure that sport is the better for their participation, and that it is left fit to be enjoyed by those who follow. Only then can we really believe that sport has a healthy future, built on the foundation of mutual respect.

Jonathan Agnew, known as Aggers, is a BBC cricket correspondent, broadcaster and writer and a former professional cricketer. Jonathan regularly writes for national newspapers and has a weekly column in Waitrose Weekend. He is married with two grown-up children.

CHAPTER ELEVEN

THE AISLEWAY CODE
Ruby Wax, on good service

I really do not know much about manners. Being American, it is not one of the top ten things to care about. As a child, I'd watch black and white English films with old crusty butlers scuttling around dressed like penguins, asking in hushed clippity-clip tones if "milady would like her ahhhhfternoooon tea seeehrved nowhooooo?". We thought, surely this couldn't be true. One of our favourite games was putting on one of these fictitious teas and pretending to be English butlers, serving our masters and bowing. At the time, my parents had a cleaning lady, an alcoholic who would try to throw a chicken leg onto your plate from the floor. That's all I knew about servitude.

When I got to this country, I was alarmed the first time I saw a queue, having absolutely no concept of why there was a line of people each facing the next person's back. This was a queue, they told me. In my country, when a bus comes we use any implement we have – including our teeth – to get to the front.

I came from the middle-class world that ruled America back in the Seventies. For us, the streets were lined with wonderful fast food restaurants. All you had to do was open your mouth and run. They had ramps leading into them, so if you were too fat to lift your legs, someone could roll you in. Then there were the all-you-can-eat-$4.99 joints. Customers took colostomy bags so when they'd filled up their own stomach, they could plug in an extension. There were salad bars long enough to land a Boeing 747 on, Eiffel Towers of tuna, and a thousand and one desserts. But then again, the US is the inventor of obesity so it makes sense. And of course, no one queued so we elbowed our way to lunch.

I arrived in Britain and after living in London for a year, ended up in Glasgow when, for some strange reason, I decided to become an actress and the city's drama school was the only one that would take me, such was my talent at the time. Back in the Seventies, there was very little electricity so it was dark most of the time. The streets were paved with people who had passed out in the night from intoxication, so we had to leap over their bodies on the way to class. The food I ate back then included fried Mars bars in a bun, old pork pie, which looked like my grandmother in a crust and toad in the hole – food pornography. And all of it served in old, stained newspaper thrown at you by someone toothless on a methadone programme.

Imagine my surprise coming from bright pink and turquoise American diners with cheerleaders on roller skates, serving shakes and root beer alight with sparklers, their lips pulled back in a smile of wall-to-wall teeth. Ten years later they brought the idea here but it never really worked. You just got depressed English waitresses looking miserable on out-of-control wheels, going "sorry, sorry, the food's not very good here" then falling over.

But then I have always said everything from America worms its way over here in about ten minutes: cream rinse, ice cubes, Botox, Jerry Springer. Every UK street corner has been Starbucked to death and each town shopping malled to the max.

Since I've lived here I've learnt to blend in and play by the rules. I suppose you could call these manners. I have learnt to say "please" and "thank you" when I need something. I give out party bags when people leave my house and, if I am invited to dinner, I write a thank-you note. "Yes, the food went in and came out again with great success. Yours, Ruby." But being polite is a dying art.

In fact if you ever had any illusion that the English are polite these days, go shopping, eat in a restaurant, stay in a hotel and have that bubble burst. No one will say, "May I help you," even if you are having a seizure.

In most high street shops you won't even see a salesperson and, if you do, he will ignore you because he is not supposed to find you clothes. He is there to look cool with his weird spiked hair and tight T-shirt. In Abercrombie and whatever, he will be topless with a six-pack and look at you like you're a disabled snail.

At the pubescent, cheaper end of the clothes market, you'll find clothes so inflammable, if you lit a cigarette the whole place would blow. My children and I shop there for exactly the same clothes. Guess which one of us is pathetic? I try to pull on the jeans made for a Barbie doll with a shoe horn. The waistline is cut so low you could give birth and not have to open the zipper. I match that with a crop top to make sure all five of my stomachs can fall out for an airing. My children threatened to divorce me last time we went shopping.

In the really cheap shops nothing hangs on hangers, it's just piles of stuff that you pick through. There are no salespeople either, only tiny girls who ask you how many clothes you're taking into the changing room. They hand you a number – that's their job. They won't ever stick their heads in and ask if you need another size. You could starve to death in those changing rooms and no one will ever come in. No one cares if you live or buy.

At the other end of the social high street – on the Bond Streets and Sloane Avenues – in the upper echelons of designer shops, you will meet the A-team of "shop bitches", as I like to call them. Stick insects who have thrown up everything they've ever eaten. Before you even get through the front door you have to get by their very own version of Checkpoint Charlie and wait while they decide whether to open the door for you. Once inside – if you get inside – it's made clear that you are nothing. You

RUBY WAX

have no meaning on Earth, according to Stick Insect. Because no matter how much you have in life, she is thinner than you. The first grenade is flung as she holds a size two in your face. "Oh, these would look really good on you, you should try them on." You ask how much and she replies, unflinching, probably in French: "Two thousand pounds. You want to try them on?"

Now you stagger into the changing room in a hail of humiliation. You are sweating and panting. The only way you can get them on is if you stick your lower half in a pencil sharpener. You can hear her out there smirking. You see yourself in the mirror from all angles and it's grotesque. But stop, right there. See if you can follow this handy manoeuvre. Lift yourself up out of the mud. Raise your chin. Breathe, breathe. Have some dignity. You can do it. Now open the changing room curtain. Come forward, stare in her dead, shark eyes and say, "My large bottom deserves better. I refuse to cover it for anything less than £4,000, thank you." Then depart. We will fight them on the beaches, we will fight them in the shops.

That's why these days I am so grateful for shopping online. No more confidence courses so I can deal with Stick Insects, now it's just a push of the button. A button can't break your self-esteem. And if your order doesn't fit, who'll know? Anything that can be done in your home without the attitude is a blessing. I'll be glad if technology

167

manages to eliminate this species. I hope they're sorry they never told me to have a nice day.

It's the same in some top-end restaurants. The only way to get service is if you are famous. Then they will carry you in off the street, wrap your coat in tissue paper and practically finger-feed you. They'll display you on the centre table like an exotic flower arrangement to show the world they have an A-lister swallowing in their establishment. I have called up saying I was Alan Rickman. That always gets me the centre table and then I pretend Alan has been taken to A&E so he can't make it.

If you are anyone else (in other words: a commoner) you will be hanging on the phone for ten years waiting to book a table at one of these establishments, which will grudgingly be given to you only if someone drops out with smallpox. The way the world is now, no one cares about your fish of the day or whether you're having a good day. Times are tough and there is no time for smalltalk. Forget those meandering conversations about the beastly weather or how horrid it is the carbuncles aren't in season.

On the surface, restaurant service in America may seem better, but don't be fooled. We have more sophisticated surf and turf eateries with gargantuan portions that can cover many plates, served by big smiling waiters who tell you about "his fish of the day" with such pride you'd think he went out and harpooned it himself. "We have a halibut that is slightly moist, roasted in the jus of its own mother, with a dribble of vin." He'll then give you his recommendations because he cares about you – but even more than you, he cares for the tip you're going to leave. And if you leave a big one, when you come back he will remember your name, the names of your kids and bring out your favourite ketchup. That's the only reason we have manners in America because we know if we give a big, big "howdy" smile – even if we're just handing you a towel in the toilet – we can expect a tip. In America, money makes manners.

I used to be a waitress at the Holiday Inn's coffee shop in Evanston, Illinois, and I was so delightful, I even read fortunes based on what people left on their plates. I'd pretend to go into a trance over some leftover egg yolk and tell people their future. Now that's service. I made more money in tips than my father ever made.

British restaurants aren't the only places that like to keep you on hold. In this country, do not expect any-one to be on the other end of the phone when you call a hotel switchboard. Room service may or may not show up, depending on their mood. And do not expect things in your room to work: flatscreen TVs, heaters, air-conditioners – anything, in fact, that has a start button – will not be connected to anything as helpful as power. The worst are the hotels with the word "Grande" in the name. That's because, in most cases, the last time they were grand was 100 years ago and since then no one has bothered cleaning.

I stayed at the finely named Majestic Hotel a few years ago and the ceiling fell in on my head while I was sleeping. They told me it happened quite often and asked if I wanted to move rooms? The next day, when I was back home, I saw on television that the hotel had burnt to the ground. I assumed that happens often too.

It can swing the other way though: you pay £600 a night to stay in an ultra-cool hotel that has no furniture in the lobby except half a giant egg and a log. You'll know the hotel has a spa because there's a photo above reception with a rock and a lit candle.

And that's another thing: English spas. In England, spa treatments usually involve a therapist in a pinkish surgeon's gown, speaking in a tiny vegetarian voice and applying dots of moisturiser with the pressure of a mosquito landing. She whispers in your ear that she's draining your lymph nodes and to drink lots of water when she's finished – as if your body even knew she was there. Then she will lead you to a room with reclining beds and lit candles to get over the remarkable experience you've just had.

In other countries when you go to a spa, you're overwhelmed by the choice: Thai, Balinese, Lomi Lomi Nui, physio floating massage, Vunkuwa African, Yin Yang tandem, alpine or Ayurvedic.

Recently in Morocco I was in a *hammam* (fancy steam room) and was met by a *tellak*, the master of the *hammam*. He began by delicately peeling off all my skin then hand-washing me. All he wore was a piece of cloth. I was expecting an *Arabian Nights* vibe but it ended more like me and mommy in the tub. He finished by taking a golden bowl and rinsed me like I was some kind of expensive rare fish.

In the UK and the US, no one much cares about you as a human being. We are all dispensable, we're not staying long. We don't know our neighbours anymore because who has time to mingle? If you had to identify any of them in a police line-up you'd never get it right. Most people have jobs not for the love of doing the work, but for survival, so as a customer you are just something to feed, sell to or hustle. Because so much is done on the phone and internet now, other people take on an unreality; they are just a voice, an image. We very rarely think about the person we're dealing with and his life, fears, dreams, hopes and frustrations. We rarely tell each other anything personal in case others think we might be weak or not up to the mark. But we will only ever become decent to each other when we realise that in order to survive, individually and as a species, we have to connect to one another on a visceral level, where we really listen, we're curious and care about each other. We have to remember that the only time we are really happy is not with bigger and bigger rewards but when we bond. We work best as a herd, not as individuals.

I hosted a retail conference a few months ago and there were very powerful people in the audience – the heads of Harvey Nichols, Urban Outfitters, Selfridges, Harrods, John Lewis, Topshop and others. Expensive business facilitators from around the world came on stage and used PowerPoint, multi-coloured graphs and firework displays to teach leaders how to engage with their employees and customers. It was all totally incomprehensible.

My job was to interview Cheryl Devil, who works on a fruit and veg stall at Portobello Road market. Her family has had a stall there for 95 years. The conference organiser thought there would be something to learn from a person who was selling face to face, especially from someone whose family has been doing it 95 years.

I've known Cheryl for 20 years. I bargain with her at her stall – sometimes having to pay only £10 for a mushroom – but I always walk away feeling good, that the deal was fantastic. That's how good she is. She is a genius at retail and when we were pregnant at the same time, the hormones made us hug and scream at each other over her bananas.

During the interview, she told me how much she loves her life-long customers. She likes to call them "Darling", "Honey Bunch" and "Lovely", even very old people. Many come to her with their problems, she gives them recipes, tells them what's in season and what goes with what.

She gets up at 4am to pick up her vegetables and then sells them until late at night. Sir Terry Leahy, the former CEO of Tesco offered her a job, as did other honchos in the audience. She turned them all down saying she loved her job and her relationship with customers. It was clear there was no substitute for someone like Cheryl, who knows how to deal with people, how to make them feel like they matter and are being heard. Technology may get so complex we can shop just by thinking about it, but if we don't get the "human" back in the driver's seat, we're doomed. We are emotional creatures and have to get some heart back into the relationship. No training can help you do that, this is something money can't buy and you can't fake. First create the relationship and if you get it right, people will give you the keys to their cars, give you their money and even marry you. Connection with others is all that matters.

Ruby Wax is a comedian and television presenter who became famous in the Eighties. Her long career has earned her a large fan base who admire her succinct and witty delivery of forthright views. She is married with three grown-up children.

CHAPTER TWELVE

THE HIGHWAY CODE
Richard Hammond, on good driving

While riding a scooter through Vietnam, I developed the idea that this chaotic, seemingly ungoverned maelstrom of motorcycles, horses and cars was founded on a balance, a naturally flourishing harmony that let people go about their business. I watched scooter riders dash madly across junctions, missing other vehicles by distances measurable only in microns and I watched as they stopped at a rare set of lights to chat with other riders and drivers alongside them − a process made easier by their unwillingness to wear any effective form of crash helmet − and I had a beautiful vision of a sort of flock intelligence, an invisible network of co-operation allowing the whole mass of people to turn and wheel about as one, without ugly rules and codes.

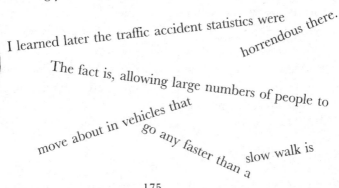

I learned later the traffic accident statistics were horrendous there. The fact is, allowing large numbers of people to move about in vehicles that go any faster than a slow walk is incredibly complicated and so fraught with peril it's a miracle the whole idea wasn't written off as a bad 'un when we got as far as the horse and cart. While my vision of a Vietnamese flock intelligence governing life on the roads turned out to be utter horse emissions, the answer doesn't lie only in rules and regulations. It is good manners that will save us all; make our lives not only safer and faster, but better, brighter, happier and longer.

And the starting point for this transformative process lies not within huge and terrible events that make the news. It all starts with the humdrum, the things we see and experience every day.

It's Thursday, 5 January, 2012, and I am driving my two daughters into Cheltenham. I've been on the receiving end of worse. I mean, we weren't in dire peril or anything. It's not as though anyone had actually tried to murder us. It was just that suddenly, nothing went my way. Every junction was filled by a van carrying, I can only imagine, a crate-load of inertia that prevented it moving the three feet required to let me in. Every gap in the traffic was suddenly occupied by a large executive car, the driver apparently unable to turn his head on his neck and see the little white Fiat and its three cheery occupants trying desperately to join the flow. But I had, as I said, experienced far worse, weirdly enough in another small, borrowed car.

Many many years earlier I borrowed my then girlfriend's Renault 5, also white, to drive to work in Black-burn, Lancashire. A bus driver had taken exception to some infringement he considered me to have committed and stopped his fully loaded school bus in the road in front of me. He leaped out, ran around the bus – bring-ing smiles of joy and anticipation to the children's faces smeared against the windows – and arrived at my car in a storm cloud of fury and spittle. As he roared and bellowed like a rutting elk, I noticed that his twisted, contorted face bore amateurishly traced tattoos depicting a dragon and a numbered barcode. I declined his offer to get out of the little Renault to discuss the matter fur-ther, and rolled up the window to prevent the unpleasant ingress of spittle loaded with, based on the heavy smell, flakes of a Ginster's pasty. This wound his fury up to a level otherwise unimaginable and he proceeded to deliver to the car the blows he so clearly desired to apply to my person. This was the point at which I figured it best to move on, and without grazing the furiously wind-milling psychopath who had only recently been at the helm of a school bus, I drove on in my girlfriend's little Renault and prepared myself to slip into the seat in a studio at BBC Radio Lancashire and welcome morning listeners to another fine day.

That ordeal, it must be said, was far worse than this morning's escapade a decade and a half later in leafy Cheltenham. I had borrowed my wife's white Fiat 500 for the trip, on account of my big, manly Landrover throwing a hissy fit in the yard and refusing to play. What tweaked and plucked at my over-stretched mental strings now was not aggression – I had encountered nothing on our short trip like the raw, naked fury unleashed on me by a crazed bus driver clearly on the verge of violence in Blackburn. It was the rudeness. I had been snubbed, shoved and bullied. A driver alongside me right at that moment had blankly refused to give me space on the road. He hadn't actually rammed me but his car body-language made it quite plain that he wanted to occupy both lanes and it wouldn't do to have some bloke in what he probably saw in his testosterone-addled noggin as a "girl's car". He had harried and bullied me out of his way and was now drawing alongside, glaring at me with dismissive contempt, as a cat might at a mouse it had recently released from under its paw. In a flash of inspiration, rather than revert to the traditional tirade of swearing and digit-waving, I turned in the seat and spoke to my daughters over my shoulder.

"Ooh girls, I know that man in the car next to us. Haven't seen him for ages. He's lovely. Give him a big wave and a smile." They duly did. The spectacle of a brace of young girls waving cheerily and blowing kisses didn't do much for the blood pressure of the ape in the car next door but it sent a giddy little smile scampering across my face. And so I had recruited my two daughters as child soldiers in this war. It had got that bad, I stooped that low. And all we were trying to do, each and every vehicle on the busy road into Cheltenham, was go about our business. So why? Why the rudeness, the barely contained aggression, the dog-eat-dog attitude leading to children being recruited to do battle and played with self-satisfied triumph as a sort of nuclear trump card?

There, I've confessed my moment of shame. It's OK though, we must all come to terms with our own conduct and face our own flaws if we are to address this. Rummage through your own mind and there's a good chance there'll be a similarly awkward memory lurking in there. If not, I salute you and you should make yourself available immediately for scientific examination because this is a problem that blights most of us every day in one way or another and it shows no sign of going away.

There is, of course, a big, angry elephant in the room: Road Rage. Because what I encountered in Blackburn, was definitely that. Road Rage. Tabloid editors love it as a headline catchphrase for reasons beyond pithy alliteration – it resonates and chimes with us all. The words themselves are potent. Roads are fundamental to us, have been for millennia, even if only to trudge home to our cave with a basket of grubs. The word "road" sings of freedom, mobility, a right, and there's a clue to its significance. A "right" to get out there and do what we all must do to support ourselves and our families and make our way through life. Civilisation itself can be seen encapsulated in the calm, ordered efficiency of a well-used, well-ordered road connecting two places together, whether a dirt track or the M4.

And "rage", well there's a word dripping with red-fanged resonance. It's rage that drives people to kill, to murder in furious vengeance or to survive in indignant fury in the face of unfair odds stacked heavily against them. Put them together and there's a potent mix indeed, and one with which we are all familiar. We've all seen it out there, watched in impotent horror as an innocent, pensionable driver is set upon verbally by some young executive thruster in a BMW because he objected to the way their naturally age-dulled reactions took fractionally longer to respond to a gap in the traffic at a T-junction than a fighter pilot might to jink left and hit the fire button. But more significant than our personal memories of witnessing Road Rage, I think, is the guilty secret that we've also all actually felt it.

In the darkest places in our hearts, we have all at some point wanted to scream, to shake, to murder the idiot in front because they're not even travelling at the speed limit and we're late to drop off our kids for their first day at school, which will put them on the back foot with their friends, ruin their confidence and lead them inevitably to a life of crime and vice. Most of us confine our fury to muttered cursing and, perhaps, a fleeting fantasy that we shall later pass the same driver by the side of the road in a cloud of steam and not stop to help them. Occasionally, and sometimes famously, it erupts into actual violence with terrible consequences. In our cars, we are somehow freed from the normal restrictions on behaviour, the sensible codes and rules that allow us to co-exist on a crowded, bustling planet.

Road Rage is an outcome, an ultimate manifestation of the lingering, seeping, all-pervading rot of bad manners. To stop it, we first must rid ourselves of bad manners because it is the everyday, seemingly insignificant moments of rudeness and inconsiderate behaviour that harden us all and dehumanise us until we recognise other drivers only as machines, see them as their cars, rather than people.

The authorities do little to help foster good manners out there. In some areas, a miserable, grey-skinned human skink in what I hope very much was a window-less, terrible cell in a council office building, banned the handing-over of our paid-for parking ticket to the next person if there was some time left to run on it. Why? This was the one occasion, often in many months, when we might get to experience the warm, simple rush of joy that comes from receiving or distributing the milk of human kindness. It's such a casual gesture, such a small thing, but it establishes a connection, an engagement that humanises the driving experience and is exactly the sort of mild but deeply significant act that would stop Road Rage in its tracks.

The authorities banned it because they realised they could get more money out of us. Once one driver leaves, another ticket must be bought and the council might double their money if there's an overlap. But if I pay to park for an hour, leave after half an hour and hand the ticket over to the next driver who stays for half an hour, the authorities have still made their money – the rent is paid for an hour. What they have done is eradicate a rare opportunity for us to behave towards one another as decent, civil human beings and the eventual cost of this tiny extra profit will be enormous when it leads to furious bus drivers hurling themselves at innocent civilians in borrowed Renaults, possibly traumatising a bus load of schoolchildren who go on to become hardened criminals and enemies of the very society that outlawed the one little act of social caring that might have avoided their exposure to violence and anger in the first instance.

And the way they stamped it out, the mechanisms involved? They make us write our registration number on the ticket and display it. They reduced us to numbers. They further dehumanised the motoring environment.

The car and the car driver – and let's get one thing straight, that is pretty much all of us, in one way or another – are an easy target. So often "the motorist" is slated in the news for their selfish and unlawful behaviour while the humble pedestrian is praised and lauded for their selfless sacrifice and fresh-air dedication. But they are the same. You drive your car, get out and walk to the shops, to work or to school. Does that make you a pedestrian or a motorist? And is it a permanent distinction, a life-altering commitment to one side or the other? Or can we agree that motorists are just people in cars, no matter how temporarily.

Of course, the act of driving round in a car is then subject to further condemnation and social analysis. Cars are condemned as status symbols and arrogant statements. Well yes, of course they are symbols. The whole process of leaving our home to go out there, into the wide world to do stuff is laden with symbolism. The car is a costume. Some will always want the biggest head-dress to display their potency, wealth and power. Others will be happier blending into the crowd. But they're making no less a statement about their personality and perceived place in the pack than the young boardroom bandit in their Beemer.

You could say it is in the car that we roam the hunting grounds for prey to bring back to our families. You could say then, it's war out there and, if it is, then manners have no place in war. We are animals. The pursuit of speed itself is about dominating territory, being the best hunter, procreating and launching our genes into the future. Yes, maybe, but it's also handy for going to the shops. The question is, can we evolve to see beyond the dog-eat-dog stuff and find a civilised way of conducting ourselves in cars? Or are we condemned forever to revert to cavemen and women as soon as we leave the drive.

By definition, driving is something we do just to get to wherever it is we need to go, unless you are a professional driver, of course. In which case, er, well let's just assume you're not for now. Our experience on the roads absolutely will and does affect the rest of our day. Encounter harsh, rude, aggressive people on the way to work and how can we be expected to sashay about the office distributing kindness and generosity towards our colleagues? Meet just one example of considerate, human behaviour on the A40 and suddenly our day is turned around, our mind softened and our hearts opened to be receptive, generous and gentle.

So I propose we adopt the following rules for modern manners on the road.

Look 'em in the eye. This gets right to the heart of the problem. We look at the vehicle, the big metal machine, not the squidgy, organic thing driving it. We are still people, it's just that we're wearing a car. I taught my daughters to always look a waiter or waitress in the eye when they ask for their food. Bikers are taught to make eye contact with car drivers whenever they can at junctions and other dodgy points where it's entirely possible you might get killed. You've seen the films where an experienced assassin tells the trainee not to look his targets in the eye before he pops a cap in their head. Well, the same principle applies here. Pushing and shoving your way into the road in a flurry of anonymous traffic is one thing, but risking the life of a fellow human being with who you have just communicated at the most basic of levels, by looking into their eyes and their soul, is an altogether different one. Of course, if someone, after being on the receiving end of your most soulful, open-hearted gaze, still pulls out on you, they are a psychopath and should be avoided at all costs.

Don't drive round the place expecting good manners from those around you. This is not a deeply cynical commentary on today's world, it's the way it should work. Nobody walks about in a crowd expecting others to open every door for them, invite them to go first at every queue for the tills or take their seat because it has a better view of the pitch. Unless they're the Queen of course, but then she generally has a driver so this whole exercise is of limited practical use for Her Majesty. The point is, expecting everyone to be perfectly courteous and well mannered is, in itself, a sort of ill-mannered behaviour. Good manners are to be welcomed with joy and sincerity when encountered, but certainly can't and shouldn't be counted upon. Everyone is in a hurry, everyone's journey is important or they wouldn't be making it. Or are we each to believe we are the only person going somewhere important? We should each drive around hoping for the opportunity to be the one whose considerate behaviour oils the wheels and makes someone else's journey that little bit easier.

We already have rules of the road. Abide by them. It is not good manners to shout in a library, to smoke on an aeroplane or to strip in a church. There are rules about such things. And there are well-established rules governing our behaviour on the roads. I'm not saying that the Highway Code is intended as a book of etiquette, but possibly the best starting point for polishing our manners on the roads is to stick to the rules that are already there. Doing so demonstrates without words that you understand you share the roads with a lot of other, equally time-pressed folk going about their business and that you must find and earn your place among them.

Do not judge people by what they drive – yes, I am aware the ice upon which I am standing is creaking a little, but bear with me. Obviously, we can and shall judge people by what they drive, but it shouldn't affect how we interact with them on the road. I can't stand pashminas and while I might think someone is just another flimsy, north London poseur wafting about in what is, essentially, a really expensive woollen scarf, I wouldn't actually barge them out of a shop doorway to get in first. A Nissan Micra might not be your kind of thing, but it should be remembered it doesn't necessarily make the driver of the one in front a drooling, incontinent old irrelevance. It's just their car. Equally, another driver might not consider a purple metalflake Citroen Saxo VTS with rusty wheel arches, a wonky spoiler and a banging stereo to be acceptable as a means of getting about, but it would be no more appropriate for them to allow their distaste for your car to influence their behaviour towards you than it would for you to leave them stranded on the cross-hatching at a lane filter because they had the temerity to leave their drive in a Volvo estate. I knew a vicar who drove a rally-spec Subaru Impreza. Think what a fool you could make of yourself by leaping to conclusions there.

Do not tailgate. Tailgating is dangerous, yes. The police tell us not to do it, as they should. But it is also indicative of a state of mind that should have the tailgater's keys removed and thrown in a skip along with the tailgater him or herself. It is straight-up bullying. I doubt if one per cent of regular tailgaters would march through a shopping centre an inch behind an innocent, unsuspecting shopper just to make the point that they can go faster. So let's agree not to do it in our cars, because it is possibly the worst and most regularly exhibited example of bad manners on the road.

Do not elect yourself as Judge Dredd and cast judgment on those around you. For example, at a point where two lanes merge into one, perhaps to accommodate roadworks, we are supposed to do just that: "merge". We should drive up to roughly the point where one lane vanishes then merge into the traffic in the remaining lane. Some drivers – often, I've noticed, truckers – decide they would prefer to move across into what will become the one surviving lane a mile or two early. That is their choice. It might be your choice though, to do as the traffic police advise, and get closer to the pinch point before merging – the alternative, they say, is that the inevitable queue simply begins a mile or two earlier, often across a roundabout or a junction, making everyone's lives worse. The point is, whatever your approach, leave others to deal with it their own way. Do not appoint yourself judge, jury and hangman and use, for instance, your truck as some sort of barrier, swinging across both lanes to prevent those wishing to merge nearer the pinch point from passing. There are laws and guidelines already in place for this situation. You may not agree with them. It is not your job to turn vigilante and enforce your own, homemade rules, whatever they are. Doing so is just rude.

Do not throw litter out of the windows. How can it even be necessary to say this, but people still do it. And it is the single worst example of bad manners, in any situation, to throw your junk where it will, at the very least, spoil the surroundings for everyone else who passes, to say nothing of causing a genuine and physical hazard, pose a risk to wildlife, cost thousands to remove and ultimately add up to making the world a worse place in a million different ways. It's the ultimate motoring sin.

Don't get indignant. People cock up all the time. We all get stuff wrong, sometimes in the kitchen, on the phone, at the computer or yes, at the wheel. He or she may not actually be a drug-crazed loon or an age-addled danger to us all, they might just have had a busy morning at home and forgotten to check before pulling out. Fury and indignation, no matter how righteous, will only make things worse. The stress will knock a few precious minutes off your own life or you'll make a fool of yourself at least. Leave 'em to it because next it's your turn to mess up.

Richard Hammond presents the BBC's Top Gear with Jeremy Clarkson and James May. He was badly injured in a stunt for the show in 2006 but, despite sustaining serious brain injuries, recovered and resumed his TV career. He also presents Total Wipeout. Richard lives in Herefordshire with his wife and two daughters.

HOW RUDE!

CHAPTER THIRTEEN

YOU'RE FIRED!
Mark Price, on business etiquette

I clearly remember being told, when I started in business 30 years ago, that cream would rise to the top. The subtext was clear – work hard, do the right things, know your place and, if you have the ability, you will rise to the position you deserve. There was order. Sir or surnames were the greetings of choice and school effortlessly blended into work. The worldwide web was yet to be commercialised and there was a divide between work and home.

Shows about business such as *The Apprentice* were a rarity and certainly not prime-time TV. A veil of mystery shrouded boardrooms and business etiquette. But all of this has changed – for better or for worse – and a new set of manners for a modern, fast-moving world needs to be considered.

Today, there's no doubt that there is more overt ambition in the workplace than was previously the case. But how to exercise ambition with good grace? With its instant access to a well-paid job or, more recently, an investment of £250,000, *The Apprentice* makes some people believe they can bludgeon their way to the top.

That coupled with an education policy that encouraged every breathing 18-year-old to go to university and we now have in this country an American-dream culture, a heady cocktail of aspiration, naked ambition and a sense of entitlement. I may be stating the obvious here, but there are only one hundred FTSE 100 companies! And yet every year our business schools and universities produce thousands of candidates desperate for the top jobs.

Let's start with Lord Sugar's testosterone-pumped apprentices. They give their teams boorish names such as Empire, Velocity, Phoenix and Sterling all the while bragging to camera, "I'm like a shark, right at the top of the food chain," or "I truly am the reflection of perfection," and, "They call me the Blonde Assassin," believing it is acceptable to trample their colleagues at any cost. If you must have a nickname, a self-deprecating one is best.

When I ran the High Wycombe branch of John Lewis, the splendid carpet department manager gave himself the nickname, Underlay. Whenever he entered the dining room, everyone called out "Underlay Underlay", like a surreal Mexican chant! It made people smile – everyone liked David.

This is the kind of thing the Mr Win types in *The Apprentice* do not understand. Naked ambition is naked bad taste. Can you imagine people calling out, "Blonde Assassin" in the same way? *The Apprentice* has stoked the fire of yob culture in the office. It is all about telling, not listening. I was once advised to ask for five pieces of information for every one you give. This wonderful guidance forces you to take an interest in the views of others and avoid the breathtaking arrogance of those who assume they have all the answers. These contestants are not role models for business or, indeed, good manners in the workplace. They promote a look-at-me culture, fuelled by an age in which celebrities are worshipped. I am pleased to say, this approach rarely works. Lord Sugar worked hard all his life for his fortune. His apprentices appear to think they need put out only 12 episodes of effort. It is no surprise that only a few of the winners work for him for long.

We all know a person who does little work in a group, but then insists on presenting. They never think of acknowledging or thanking the team, a cornerstone of good manners in business. They go above the boss's head to promote their credentials and, worst of all, knowingly allow a colleague to fail to feather their own nest. You meet them at parties looking for a more important person to talk to. They talk about their life's work and ambitions at a business dinner, but fail to ask you even the most basic of questions. It really is all about them. They wouldn't have the self-confidence to admit a mistake or say sorry, both of which are the height of good manners.

If you are fabulously successful, work colleagues do not want to hear about your yacht or ski chalet. A colleague made the fatal mistake of explaining he had travelled to a sporting event by helicopter. At every subsequent meeting the poor chap was teased mercilessly whenever a helicopter flew past with jokes about whether his pick-up was early.

Good manners require you not to flaunt your worldly wealth. If asked what car you drive simply say, "a green one". Whenever anyone asks me about my position, I reply: "Standing up!" It is perfectly acceptable to burst the bombastic bubble of those self-aggrandisers. At a recent party, a retail multi-millionaire was boasting about his garden, saying it took almost half a day to mow. I couldn't help but quip that I used to have an unreliable old mower too!

Further fuel on this bonfire of self-promoted vanity is the notion that hard work can get anyone to the top. It doesn't matter how hard I train, I couldn't beat Usain Bolt in the 100 metres. I simply don't have the physiology or DNA. The whole point of working hard is to be the best you can be.

The flames of this American dream have been fanned by a staggering increase in the number of university graduates. And what's the result? False hope and, ultimately, disappointment for the majority, followed by a feeling of resentment, which undermines the status quo. Few think they can play centre-forward for England so they don't begrudge the player his fortunes, and yet many stare up the business chain thinking: "I could do that." The best route to business progression is doing your job consistently well, the opposite to the Snakes and Ladders antics seen on *The Apprentice*.

Obviously, I'm not saying you shouldn't be ambitious and I'm not saying you needn't work hard: hard work is good and so is ambition. But my advice is to refrain from telling everyone you plan to be MD. Just calmly set out your aspirations, acknowledging strengths and weaknesses that need to be addressed, then get your head down and do your job to the best of your ability. Be sensible in your time horizons. Telling the boss you intend to get his job in double-quick time is poor form. And remember, you are not competing against your colleague, but against yourself.

Business is and always was about the team and leaders can lead only because they are liked and respected by the people they manage. A management style that relies on generating a sense of fear is not leadership, it is autocracy. Your friends wouldn't wear it so why should your colleagues?

In Waitrose, which is part of the John Lewis Partnership, all 50,000 employees are co-owners. The founder of the Partnership, John Spedan Lewis, believed that if his employees shared in the profits; were given information on how their company was doing and the power to influence its direction, they would give more. As a consequence customers would feel valued and commercial success would follow in a virtuous circle. So in Waitrose and John Lewis we are all fellow owners and as such respect each other whatever our positions. Mistakes are seen as a way of learning and gaining experience, NOT hanging offences.

This approach has led Waitrose and John Lewis to become two of the most loved brands in Britain because the Partnership has been able to accept when things have gone wrong, has not defended mistakes and has then moved heaven and Earth to put them right. If this humble approach of being heroic in recovery works for a whole business, it certainly should work for an individual.

Ever-changing technology has changed the business landscape beyond recognition and so we should probably adjust our expectations of workplace manners as a consequence. Thanks to the worldwide web and mobile telephones, we live in a world in which everyone is important, where everyone can be "friends" with anyone. We pronounce even our most humdrum thoughts on Twitter and our Facebook pages are poised, ready to host any and all of our latest musings.

This is a humongous change that requires us to answer some questions. Should personal emails or texts be sent at work? Should mobile devices be checked in a meeting? Is it acceptable to leave a meeting to answer a call? Is shopping online a suitable pursuit in the office?

What is the etiquette for interrupting colleagues who are
working on their PCs or on the phone? With BlackBerrys
a seemingly essential part of office kit, should you reply
to emails during out-of-office hours? Is it acceptable to
delete the millions of unsolicited mails and texts received?
Should you protest at being copied into the most trivial
email circulated to all and sundry?

Where on Earth to start? Well, as always with manners,
consideration for others comes first. When that is missing,
sadly, rules must be applied. But if a company needs to
offer guidance on how people should treat each other, it
implies its employees are not all that nice. It is easier to
train nice people than train people to be nice. On a recent
visit to Japan, I was quite put out when the president of a
major corporation met me wearing a surgical face mask.
He didn't want to catch my germs, I thought.

Afterwards, I explained my disappointment to the
translator. She was shocked, and said the president had a
cold, and had worn the mask to protect colleagues from
his germs. It was out of respect, she said. Contrast that
with some offices where, in order not to be disturbed
while working at your desk, I've been told that employees
wear a baseball cap. To me, all this illustrates is there is
no respect for others who are busy and that the only way
to ward off colleagues is to wear a hat. Not only a hat,
but a hat indoors, and a vulgar baseball cap best left to
fans of the sport popular on the other side of the Atlantic.

Whatever happened to good old sensitivity to the needs of others? (And anyway, if you have to wear a hat, surely a British deerstalker or top hat would be more appropriate in this country?) The fact that an office is open-plan should not signal the green light that everyone is entitled to permanent access to everybody else.

It is not acceptable to email or text in a meeting, unless it is an emergency. It's discourteous. I certainly don't allow it in any meeting I chair. Could you imagine having an audience with the Queen and chatting to your friends via text while you were doing so? No, you wouldn't. Therefore you must assume if someone does email or text in a meeting, they think they are more important than the others attending. And that's just rude. I am totally bemused by my daughters' generation who arrange to meet each other but then spend the entire time communicating with friends they are not seeing. I fear for the art of conversation and really getting to know people.

Having said all that, I do think it is acceptable to send personal emails and texts – or even do your online shop – at work if it counts towards your break time. I also think modern communications have rendered it quite the norm to email or phone colleagues out of work hours. But it is important to remember they are not obliged to respond until they return to work.

The main issue with email, though, is that it is now much easier and cheaper for customers and suppliers to contact businesses. Every hour of every day, there is a torrent of communication in place of a quality trickle. It can take an executive an entire day to answer emails so there is little alternative but to delete circulars without response. I am amazed how often I get emails about stationery supplies or a new marketing idea. They are addressed to the wrong person and I delete them immediately. Campaigning emails that arrive in their thousands from special interest groups also end up in the trash folder, after I have read the first one and usually posted a response on the website. I also think it is acceptable to forward customer emails to customer services, a team which has been set up specifically for the purpose of dealing efficiently and courteously with queries. This means there is time to craft a courteous reply to emails from people with whom you do have a business relationship. It is an illusion to think that you deserve a response just because you pinged an email to an address you found on a website. Relationships in business require time and effort.

The ease with which employees of larger companies can be copied in on emails contributes to this inbox explosion. It is a poor and thoughtless habit and, if you are minded, you must reply to the sender asking why on Earth they felt the need to include you in their round robin. Perhaps the sender thought copying in all and sundry would excuse them in the event of things going wrong; that the single act of sending an email would abdicate them from any responsibility? But that's like whispering something in a corner of an office then saying later you definitely raised the subject in the building. Have the self-confidence to make a decision and then learn from any mistake. I remember seeing a young graduate who had mistakenly ordered 10,000 packs of beef burgers rather than the 1,000 that was supposed to be ordered. The mistake cost us many thousands of pounds in excess wastage and the poor grad offered a resignation. But I immediately declined having spent a vast amount on training.

The internet and the resulting 24-hour news culture have created an environment in which people believe they have a right to any information at any time. Inspired perhaps by Jeremy Paxman's interrogative style on *Newsnight*, and emboldened by the arrogant ambition on *The Apprentice*, people seeking out information they "need to know" do so without a thought for anyone else. But someone must respond to their endless requests and usually that's down to beleaguered bosses and managers. Most of the time, those requests come from well-meaning members of staff stuck in bad habits.

But I have seen the act of asking questions and seeking clarification used as a tool by the over-ambitious to get noticed. Indeed, it does get them noticed, but usually for the wrong reasons, while more diligent, respectful colleagues quietly get on producing the results needed in a successful business.

In a nutshell, emails and texts are too easy. Before pressing send, think twice about what you expect the recipient to do and in what time frame. And remember yours might not be the only or most important mail they receive that day.

But it is not just the quantity of emails I take issue with, it's the quality too. In an email, it is important to be as formal as in a letter. Start with "Dear ..." and use the appropriate sign-off. Text speak is never acceptable. "C U L8TR" is best left to teenagers. All business communication should be as efficient as possible to speed the reader along but missing out vowels and adding acronyms only add to the task.

There are also occasions when an email is totally inappropriate: for example a texted "thank you" is just not good enough. There is no greater joy than sending and receiving a hand-written letter. Extra work but worth it. And the fact that some companies give employees their notice via text shows how far civility has fallen as a result of the worldwide web. Electronic communications can be a speedy and efficient tool, but used badly it has the opposite effect of being a hindrance.

The explosion of digital technology has had other far-reaching consequences – for instance, the ability of staff to work anywhere in the world and still be in direct com-

munication. In an effort to reduce costs and improve flex-
ibility many businesses have started to encourage working from home. This seemingly straightforward move has
blurred the line between home and work life creating a
number of new issues, chiefly a relaxed or even slobbish
behaviour transferred from home to office.

To begin, there is the vexed subject of what to
wear. Home-working has led to dress-down Fridays
and, in some cases, dress down every day. Across the
Atlantic, it is common to see techies heading to work
at global brands in Bermuda shorts and flip flops. And
it appears the question of what warrants suitable attire
affects other areas of life too: recently a branch of Tesco
needed to remind its customers not to do their weekly
shop in pyjamas! I wonder how many people working
from home do so in bedroom attire. To my mind, answering emails in pyjamas at the breakfast table may be OK (if
you are alone, of course) but by 11am it definitely is not.

On sunny days in the office there is often so much
flesh on show you'd be forgiven for confusing it with
Brighton beach. A display of décolletage is not for the
workplace unless it happens to be a lap-dance club. The
same can be said for teenage boys who wear their trou-
sers so far down their bottoms most of their underpants
are on display. Informality of dress fosters informality in
relationships. Table manners and eating habits are also
victims of the blurred lines between home and work life.

What now is the difference between the two – a sandwich on your lap at home, TV blaring, or a bite in front of the computer at work? Businesses have tried to make the workplace more homely. Soft furnishings, TVs and even table football are commonplace. Staff dining rooms now look more like mock piazza cafes in some hip advertising agencies. All well and good, but if you must eat at your desk use a napkin, sweep away the crumbs and then clear the dirty plates immediately. For your neighbour's sake if not your own.

It is my belief that a relaxed attitude at work erodes basic good manners. It may well be frustrating to see lift doors slide open for a third time for someone else to push in but offices work best when the people in them are in harmony. And that starts with mutual respect. If you pass someone in the corridor you should not amble past, head down, but say hello or nod in acknowledgment. Listening to your iPod at home is fine. It is disrespectful in the office.

Ultimately, we have to decide if we want a more in-formal home-like atmosphere – born from the intimate relationships we foster there – transferred to the office. Personally, I'd say no to that. At work there is a need to be civil and respectful while at home there is scope for warmth and love. How can you conduct an objective personal review if your relationship with a colleague is similar to the one you share with family.

Modern business methods may have changed but they

still require you to think about others and be sensitive to their needs and wants. This is simple good manners and good manners are timeless.

Mark Price has been managing director of Waitrose, the food shops of the John Lewis Partnership, since 2007. He started his career with the partnership as a graduate trainee, working his way through the ranks. Mark lives in Dorset with his wife and two daughters.

ACKNOWLEDGMENTS

My first experience of the legendary John Lewis Partnership service was when my three-year-old daughter decided to make an early bid for freedom in the frozen food aisle of Waitrose in Abingdon, Oxfordshire.

As she hot-toddled right towards fruit and veg, I lost sight of her and took a swerve left into beers, wines and spirits. The next five minutes felt more like 50, but I knew I'd found my spiritual supermarket when over the loudspeaker came a friendly, calm voice inviting "Grace's mummy to make her way to the customer service desk", where I finally found the runaway being fussed over by two lovely ladies, a carton of juice in one chubby fist and a lolly in the other.

Wind forward 15 years and in one of those strange twists of fate I'm working at Waitrose and know from experience that simple acts of kindness like this – small and large – happen in our shops, depots and offices every day. It was the belief of the John Lewis Partnership's founder, John Spedan Lewis, that if the people employed in a business had a stake in that business they would be happier and more fulfilled in their work – which, in turn, would encourage better service for customers.

This autumn, Waitrose has been part of the John Lewis Partnership for 75 years, and while no one here would claim this makes us expert in the matter of manners, we thought it would be stimulating – and fun – to celebrate our anniversary by looking at what manners do maketh in the 21st century.

It's been a fascinating project to work on and, as you can imagine, one that has involved the skills and talents of many people... which leads me nicely, I hope, to show that my mum and dad instilled good manners in me by saying thank you to everyone involved.

First, thank you to all the authors for their great writing, provocative views and challenging suggestions for new approaches to modern manners and to the illustrator Michel Streich for bringing those views to life.

Next, a huge thank you to all the team here at Waitrose headquarters in Bracknell, Berkshire: our managing director, Mark Price, for suggesting a book on modern manners in the first place; Christine Watts, for her invaluable support and encouragement; Sally Williams and Rachel Barrett for their amazing creative talents in designing the look and feel of the book; Jo Dorrell for her patience with our many changes and for making sure the pages got off to the printer in time; Claire Boother and Freya Wright for ensuring that the book arrived safely and beautifully presented in our shops; Cleland Thom for his sound advice; Angus Morrison for his expert eyes; Kim Lacey for her eagle eyes, unwavering help and support and last, but certainly not least; Alison Hepworth, for her great ideas and sound advice, her relentless determination to check every word − and for keeping me sane.

Finally, a big thank you to you, our customers: first for buying our book and then for giving it your valuable time. We really hope you enjoyed reading it.

Olwen Rice, Editor
Autumn 2012

BIBLIOGRAPHY

Ashford, Daisy. *The Young Visiters* or *Mr Salteena's Plan.* Chatto and Windus, 1919

Belloc, Hilaire. *Jim: Who ran away from his Nurse, and was eaten by a Lion, Cautionary Tales for Children.* Eveleigh Nash, 1907

Clinton, Hillary. *It Takes a Village: And Other Lessons Children Teach Us*, Simon & Schuster, 1996

Emerson, Ralph Waldo. *The Conducts of Life.* Boston, Ticknor and Fields, 1860

Feinberg, Joel. *The Moral Limits of the Criminal Law* (series). Oxford University Press, 1984–1988

Hume, David. *An Enquiry Concerning the Principles of Morals*, Oxford University Press, 1751 (new edition 1987)

Molière (Poquelin, Jean-Baptiste). *The Bourgeois Gentleman.* Ivan R Dee, 1670 (new edition 2000)

Muir, Hugh. Angry Britain: why are we becoming so intolerant? *The Guardian*, 6 December 2011

Travers, PL. *Mary Poppins*. HarperCollins, 1934

www.cbc.ca. CBC Documentary Discussion, Rude: Where Are Our Manners?, 2008

www.lottemullan.com. Mullan, Lotte, The side boob hug, 12 May 2008

REFERENCES

Carry On Up the Khyber, Dir. Gerald Thomas, The Rank Organisation, 1968

Clinton, Bill. US welfare reform campaign, 1997

Dad's Army, BBC, 1968–77

Downton Abbey, Carnival Films, 2010–

Frasier, CBS Television Distribution, 1993–2004

Jack and Jill, Dir. Dennis Dugan, Columbia Pictures, 2011

Jerry Maguire, Dir. Cameron Crowe, TriStar Pictures, 1996

Highlander II: The Quickening, Dir. Russell Mulcahy, Inter-star/Republic Entertainment/Seymour Borde & Associates, 1991

McCullough, David. Wellesley High School address to leavers, 1 June 2012

No More Heroes, The Stranglers, United Artists, 1977

Newsnight, BBC News, 1980–

Pearl Harbor, Dir. Michael Bay, Touchstone Pictures, 2001

Sex and the City, CBS Television Distribution, 1998–2004

Six Million Dollar Man, ABC, 1974–78

The Apprentice, Boundless, 2005–

The Frost Report, BBC, 1966–67

The Simpsons, Little Girl in the Big Ten, 20th Century Television, 2002

The Thin Man, Dir. WS Van Dyke, Metro-Goldwyn-Mayer, 1934

To Catch A Thief, Dir. Alfred Hitchcock, Paramount Pictures, 1955

Unequal Opportunities with John Humphrys, BBC, 2010

Yes, Minister, BBC, 1980–84

Thank you for reading me.